Brief Integrated Motivational Intervention

Brief Integrated Motivational Intervention

A Treatment Manual for Co-occurring Mental Health and Substance Use Problems

Hermine L. Graham, Alex Copello, Max Birchwood, and Emma Griffith

WILEY Blackwell

Library of Congress Catalog Number: 2016024932

Paperback ISBN: 9781119166658

A catalogue record for this book is available from the British Library.

Cover image: Gettyimages/ImpaKPro

Set in 11/14pt Legacy Serif by SPi Global, Pondicherry, India
Printed and bound in Malaysia by Vivar Printing Sdn Bhd

1   2016

To Chloe and Niamh (HG)
To my family and friends (EG)

Contents

About the Companion Website xi
About the Authors xii
Acknowledgments xv

1 Introduction 1

A Window of Opportunity 1
Brief Integrated Motivational
    Intervention (BIMI) 4
    Approach 4
    Timing 4
    Structure 5

2 Getting Started: Engagement and Brief Assessment 8

Staying Motivated 8
STEP 1: Building Engagement and Assessment 9
Session One Overview 10
Session One Outline 10
    BIMI Brief Assessment 12
    Generating the Personalized Assessment
      Feedback Sheet 31
Session Two Overview 36
Session Two Outline 36
Frequently Asked Questions (FAQs) 42
    Alcohol 43
    Drugs and Mental Health 46
    Additional Resources 52

3 Making Decisions About Change 53

How to Decide on the Next STEP 53
*How to Decide What STEP Is Appropriate
for the Client* 53
STEP 2: Making Decisions with Your Client 56
Outline of Sessions 57
Identifying the "Benefits" of Using 57
*Identifying Positive Thoughts and Mis-held
Beliefs About Alcohol and Drugs* 58
Taking Another Look at What You Think
About Alcohol and Drugs 60
Relationship Between Mental Health
Problems and Substance Use 62
Reviewing Any "Costs" of Using 65

4 Change 69

STEP 3: Change Plans and Social Support 69
Outline of Sessions 71
Taking Steps Toward My Goals 71
Coping with Setbacks 72
Strategies to Cope with Cravings and Urges 73
Social Support for Change 75
Developing Supportive Social Networks 76
Outline of Sessions 76
Helpful Information for Family Members
or Supportive Social Network Members 78
*Understanding Cannabis, Alcohol, and Other
Substance Use, and How It Impacts
on Family and Others* 79
Do Others Experience Similar Problems? 80
How Do I Make Sense of This? 80
Why Do I Feel So Stressed? 81

To Sum It Up   82

*How Can I Best Support My Family Member
or Friend?*   83

5 Boosting Change   85

Booster Session Content   85

Booster Session Outline   86

*Review Self-Motivational Statements of
Concern and Intention to Change*   87

*Review the Maintenance Cycle for Mental
Health Problems and Substance Use*   87

*Review Progress with Substance-related Goal
and Skills to Tackle Setbacks*   88

Review Social Support for Change   88

Link in with Community-based Substance
Misuse Treatment Services   89

APPENDIX   Worksheets and Handouts 90

Worksheet 1: What Do I Enjoy About Using
or What Keeps Me Using?   97

Worksheet 2: What I Enjoy About Using
or What Keeps Me Using (Table)   99

Worksheet 3: How Does My Use
Sometimes Affect Me?   100

Worksheet 4: Taking Steps Toward My Goal   101

Handout 1: Helpful Information
for Family Members or Supportive
Social Network Members   102

*Understanding Cannabis, Alcohol, and Other
Substance Use, and How It Impacts
on Family and Others*   102

Do Others Experience Similar Problems?   103

How Do I Make Sense of This?   104

Why Do I Feel So Stressed?   105

To Sum It Up   105

Handout 2: How Can I Best Support

My Family Member or Friend?   107

Keeping Communication Open   107

Supporting His or Her Goals   107

References   108

Index   115

About the Companion Website

This book is accompanied by a companion website:

www.wiley.com/go/graham/bimi

The website includes:

Handouts and worksheets

About the Authors

Hermine L. Graham is a consultant clinical psychologist and lecturer at the University of Birmingham, United Kingdom. She has expertise in cognitive behavioral therapy, and has led the development and research of service models and treatment approaches for people with severe mental health and co-occurring alcohol and drug problems in Birmingham. This work has been highlighted as a model of "good practice," and is referenced in national policy guidelines for the treatment of "dual diagnosis" (DOH, 2002). She has published widely in peer-reviewed academic journals and is co-author of *Cognitive-Behavioral Integrated Treatment (C-BIT): A Treatment Manual for Substance Misuse in People with Severe Mental Health Problems* (Wiley, 2004) and co-editor of *Substance Misuse in Psychosis: Approaches to Treatment and Service Delivery* (Wiley, 2003).

Alex Copello is a professor of addiction research at the School of Psychology at the University of Birmingham, United Kingdom, and a consultant clinical psychologist with the Birmingham and Solihull Mental Health NHS Foundation Trust. His career has combined clinical and academic work, and his research has had a major impact on addiction treatment in the United Kingdom in recent years. He has been widely published in academic scientific journals and has authored and edited many books, including *Social Behavior and Network Therapy for Alcohol Problems* (Routledge, 2009); *Coping with Alcohol and Drug Problems: The Experiences of Family Members in Three Contrasting Cultures* (Routledge, 2005); *Cognitive-Behavioral Integrated Treatment (C-BIT): A Treatment Manual for Substance Misuse in People with Severe Mental Health Problems* (Wiley, 2004); and *Substance Misuse in Psychosis: Approaches to Treatment and Service Delivery* (Wiley, 2003).

Max Birchwood is a professor of youth mental health at the University of Warwick, United Kingdom. He pioneered the concept and practice of early intervention in psychosis and opened the UK's first early intervention in psychosis service in 1994. He has published widely in the field of psychosis and is the author of many books, including *Early Intervention in Psychosis: A Guide to Concepts, Evidence and Interventions* (Wiley, 2000); *Cognitive Therapy for Delusions, Voices and Paranoia* (Wiley, 1996); *A Casebook of Cognitive Behavior Therapy for Command Hallucinations: A Social Rank Theory Approach* (Routledge, 2005); *Cognitive-Behavioral Integrated Treatment (C-BIT): A Treatment Manual for Substance Misuse in People with Severe Mental Health Problems* (Wiley, 2004); and *Substance Misuse in Psychosis: Approaches to Treatment and Service Delivery* (Wiley, 2003).

Emma Griffith is a Lecturer and Clinical Tutor for the Doctorate in Clinical Psychology at the University of Bath, UK, and also works as a Principal Clinical Psychologist in Avon and Wiltshire

Partnership Mental Health NHS Trust. She is accredited as a Behavioural and Cognitive Psychotherapist in CBT by the British Association for Behavioural & Cognitive Psychotherapies (BABCP). She has published a number of journal articles and is the co-author of a book chapter.

Acknowledgments

The research trial that evaluated the Brief Integrated Motivational Intervention program was funded by the National Institute for Health Research (NIHR)— Research for Patient Benefit research grant (PB-PG-1010-23138), and sponsored by Birmingham and Solihull Mental Health NHS Foundation Trust (BSMHFT). We are thankful for the invaluable input from Nick Freemantle and Paul McCrone as co-applicants in the research trial, and grateful to Latoya Clarke, Kathryn Walsh, and Chrysi Stefanidou for their involvement as research associates. We greatly appreciate the support and involvement of the inpatient and community staff and service users in BSMHFT who were willing to trial the approach. Special thanks are owed to Jon Kennedy and Gary Roberts for their openness to us piloting the approach on the inpatient units, and to the members of the COMPASS program team (Jo Leci, Rob O'Brien, David Ryan, Catherine Henry, Helen Tuffey, Debbie Boulton, Sue Middleton, and Gemma Martin) and Dionne Harleston for their input into drafts of the manual and for being willing to trial the treatment approach. We also appreciate the input of Blessing Marandure on the effects of cannabis on mental health and Greg Griffith for producing Figure 2.1. Finally, we thank the service user researchers and consultants for ensuring this treatment approach was relevant.

CHAPTER ONE

Introduction

▶ A Window of Opportunity

In healthcare settings, a number of opportunities to talk to clients about health-related behaviors (e.g., tobacco, alcohol, or drug use) are often "missed," which may have indirectly contributed to them being admitted or referred for treatment (e.g., Buchbinder, Wilbur, Zuskov, Mclean & Sleath, 2014). Often viewed as "precontemplators," these clients do not recognize their behavior as causing any problems or as the primary presenting problem. However, it has been suggested that such occasions—that is, when problems are acute—represent "teachable moments" (e.g., Lau et al., 2010; Buchbinder et al., 2014) that present staff in healthcare settings with natural "windows of opportunity" to start conversations about behaviors that may have indirectly impacted on their clients' physical and mental health (Graham, Copello, Birchwood et al., 2016). As such, there exists a significant need for brief interventions that can be delivered in inpatient or acute healthcare settings, when clients who are not necessarily motivated to talk about their substance

Brief Integrated Motivational Intervention: A Treatment Manual for Co-occurring Mental Health and Substance Use Problems, First Edition. Hermine L. Graham, Alex Copello, Max Birchwood, and Emma Griffith.
© 2016 John Wiley & Sons, Ltd. Published 2016 by John Wiley & Sons, Ltd.
Companion Website: www.wiley.com/go/graham/bimi

abuse are more "open" to considering their use. This period can be viewed as a "window of opportunity" to help clients gain insight into the role of substance use in triggering acute mental health symptoms or hospital admissions, and to improve their engagement in treatment.

Drug and alcohol use and misuse are common in clients who experience severe mental health problems (Regier et al., 1990; Mueser et al., 2000; Graham et al., 2001; Swartz et al., 2006). Substance misuse in this population has been found to be associated with poorer engagement in treatment, more symptoms and relapses, and poor treatment outcomes (Mueser et al., 2000; Graham et al., 2001; Swartz et al., 2006). In addition, these clients often express low motivation to change their drug and alcohol use (McHugo, Drake, Burton & Ackerson, 1995; Carey, 1996; Swanson, Pantalon & Cohen, 1999), and are often poorly engaged in treatment, which forms a significant barrier for change and good treatment outcomes (Mueser, Bellack & Blanchard, 1992; Swanson et al., 1999; Drake et al., 2001; Mueser, 2003). Drug and alcohol misuse have also been found to be associated with increased psychiatric hospital admissions, and seems to have a negative impact on inpatient stays (Lai & Sitharthan, 2012). Therefore, unsurprisingly, 22–44% of those admitted in the United Kingdom into psychiatric inpatient facilities for mental health problems have been found to also have coexisting alcohol or drug problems (DOH, 2006). In the United Kingdom, national health policy guidance has pointed to the need to train staff to improve routine assessment and treatment of substance misuse as part of the clinical management strategy of a psychiatric admission (DOH, 2006). Nonetheless, this has remained a significant gap in service provision (DOH, 2006; Healthcare Commission, 2008), and this natural window of opportunity is often missed.

As the acute symptoms of mental ill health decline for an inpatient, this can be a time of contemplation, when he or she reflects on how they "ended up in hospital." It may be a window of increased awareness and insight into the factors that contributed to him or her becoming unwell and/or being admitted in a hospital. However, this increased "insight" may result in increased emotional distress, and some research has shown that post-discharge is a time when individuals may "seal over" the experience, in an attempt to reduce emotional distress. That is, the inpatient may deny or minimize any recent mental health symptoms or experiences and precipitating factors, because they may be too upsetting to think about. As a result, he or she may lose awareness of the triggers for becoming unwell (Tait, Birchwood & Trower, 2003). Sealing over the experience of relapse was found to predict low engagement with services 6 months after discharge for inpatients (Tait et al., 2003). However, we know that engagement in treatment is key to improving treatment outcomes for mental health clients (Carey, 1996; Swanson et al., 1999).

The Brief Integrated Motivational Intervention (BIMI) seeks to target this window of contemplation. It provides clinicians with a brief, targeted, easy-to-use intervention that motivates people who experience mental health problems to engage in treatment and make changes in their substance use (Graham, Copello, Griffith et al., 2015). The approach seeks to raise awareness of the impact of drugs and alcohol on mental health. BIMI is empirically grounded in cognitive behavioral therapy (e.g., Beck, Wright, Newman & Liese, 1993; Greenberger & Padesky, 1995) and motivational interviewing (e.g., Hettema, Steele & Miller, 2005). It draws on the initial phases of the longer-term integrated treatment approach C-BIT (Graham et al., 2004), and on developments in the use of brief interventions in the treatment of substance use in those who experience severe mental health problems (Carey, Carey, Maisto & Purnine, 2002; Kavanagh et al., 2004; Edwards et al., 2006; Kay-Lambkin, Baker, Kelly, Lewin & Carr, 2008; Baker et al., 2009). It reflects the research evidence on increasing engagement and motivating behavior change in those with co-morbid mental health and substance misuse. BIMI was initially developed and piloted in a randomized controlled trial in acute mental health inpatient settings and has demonstrated positive outcomes for engaging inpatients with severe mental health problems in addressing their drug and alcohol use (Graham, Copello, Griffith et al., 2015).

▶ Brief Integrated Motivational Intervention (BIMI)

Approach

BIMI is designed to be delivered by routine mental health staff or specialist practitioners. This treatment manual provides a framework, session content, illustrative case material, and easy-to-use worksheets that can be used when delivering it. BIMI promotes a practical conversational style that seeks to build a good collaborative working relationship as you work together toward the client's self-identified goals. It is targeted in its approach and is recommended to take place over a brief period, ideally *2 weeks*. Sessions can range from *one to a maximum of six*, depending on the client, and are intended to be delivered in short bursts, *each of 15–30 minutes* duration. The evaluation of BIMI was performed by staff members who were trained in the approach and who received case supervision. The evaluation found that, on average, an inpatient received *three sessions*, in addition to the initial assessment session, each of an *average duration of 17 minutes*, and that the total time that clinicians (i.e., nurses, occupational therapists, healthcare assistants, activity workers, specialist dual-diagnosis clinicians) spent receiving the intervention was *57 minutes* over the *2-week period*. This short-burst approach was found to be sufficient to produce improved engagement in substance misuse treatment and some behavior change (Graham, Copello, Griffith et al., 2015). The number of sessions and their duration would best be determined by the needs of the client. Small amounts of information can be discussed in sessions, and it is helpful to provide frequent reflections and summaries of key points talked about during the sessions. Information can be presented in a number of ways (e.g., verbal, written).

Timing

The primary aim of the treatment approach is to quickly engage clients in meaningful change talk about their alcohol or drug use. BIMI is provided relatively early on in the treatment process (e.g., within the first few weeks of an inpatient's stay in hospital or when presenting at mental health services when acutely unwell). The idea is to maximize the potential of this *window of opportunity* and *teachable moment*. This would enable the intervention to take place when problems are acute and clients are "primed" to consider health issues. At this point, the clients are considered to be more cognitively open to engage in considering the links between the issue that led to them being referred or admitted and other health-related behaviors. By providing a few minutes of quiet time, over a short period, clients can reflect on their use of drugs and alcohol and start to consider the impact of such use on their physical and mental health. The timing is key and balanced with the initial acute symptoms subsiding and it being considered clinically appropriate.

Structure

BIMI uses a simple three-step framework (see Table 1.1 for an overview of the structure). The initial step (STEP 1) involves carrying out a brief assessment and then providing clients with personalized feedback of the information gathered in this assessment. The feedback details the clients' patterns of substance use and highlights its potential impacts on their physical and mental health. It is also recommended that clients be provided with individually tailored psychoeducational material/leaflets about the substance(s) they are using. The second step (STEP 2) aims to help clients make decisions about what outcomes/goals they want. This involves using strategies aimed at: increasing awareness of the perceived "benefits" of use and reflection on the "costs" associated with *continued* substance misuse; re-evaluation of positive thoughts and beliefs about substances that promote use; and building awareness of how substance use and mental health may interact and worsen each other by identifying a maintenance/vicious cycle. The third step (STEP 3) encourages clients to contemplate change and develop a change plan based on a self-identified goal, using goal planning. This helps in making change feel possible and achievable. Included are also strategies to cope with setbacks, cravings, and urges, and to provide social support for change. Not all the steps in BIMI need to be delivered. The essential step is STEP 1. The main idea is to

Table 1.1 Overview of BIMI.

Session Content	Session Goals
STEP 1: Building Engagement and Assessment Carry out brief assessment and score questionnaires Provide personalized feedback to the client from the assessment regarding: ■ Levels of use ■ Identify the client's thoughts and feelings about the personalized assessment feedback ■ Potential impact of substance use on mental health Provide material regarding: ■ Drug and alcohol use and national patterns/norms ■ Impact of alcohol and drug use on mental health, functioning, and relapse	■ Engagement and building rapport ■ Gathering information about client's substance use to build awareness about its impact ■ Ensuring awareness of the impact of substance use on mental health ■ Identifying issues for next session(s)
STEP 2: Making Decisions with Your Client ■ Identify benefits and costs of using for the present and future, and which of these are most important to the client ■ Identify positive/mis-held thoughts and beliefs about substance use that promote or maintain use ■ Identify positive/mis-held thoughts and beliefs about mental health and how it interacts with substance use ■ Begin to discuss how mental health problems and substance use may interact and worsen each other ■ Draw out a maintaining cycle of the triggers for drug/alcohol use and the impact of substance use on mental health and functioning ■ Identify self-motivational statements of concern and intent to change	■ Engagement and building rapport ■ Being able to talk openly about costs and benefits of using ■ Building recognition of how positive/mis-held beliefs may promote use ■ Recognizing maintenance cycle for mental health problems and substance use ■ Being able to state concerns about continued use and state intent to change
STEP 3: Change Plans and Social Support Developing a change plan: ■ Identify a realistic substance-related goal and/or personal goal that cutting down or quitting would help the client achieve ■ Look at motivation to change substance use and achieve the goal ■ Identify how "important" changing is and how "confident" the client feels about making changes ■ Develop an action plan ■ Identify skills to cope with cravings, urges, and triggers for use Social support for change: ■ Identify social supports that can encourage attempts to change substance misuse ■ Draw social network diagram	■ Helping to feel that change is possible ■ Identifying potential setbacks (e.g., cravings/urges and social network) ■ Being able to use skills to cope with setbacks including cravings, urges, and triggers for use ■ Providing social support for change

> **Box 1.1**   In Between Sessions
>
> After the second session, encourage participants to:
>
> 1. Access websites offering information about alcohol (e.g., "Down your Drink") and drugs (e.g., "Talk to Frank") in between each session
>
> 2. Read specific psychoeducational information regarding alcohol and drug use and their impacts

Table 1.2   Booster Session Content.

Session Content	Session Goals
Boosting Change ■ Review self-motivational statements of concern and intent to change ■ Review action plan ■ Review social support for change and introduce to community-based treatment	■ Consolidating motivation and transfer skills from BIMI to the community ■ Reviewing progress with substance-related goal and skills to tackle setbacks ■ Linking client with community-based substance misuse treatment

engage clients in the step suitable for them, so that they can meaningfully talk about and re-evaluate their alcohol or drug use (see Box 1.1, page 7, for an overview of how to decide which step is best suited). If necessary, and if the setting allows, a "booster session" (see Table 1.2) can be offered 1 month after the last session to help consolidate motivation and ensure that clients have the skills and strategies necessary to access longer-term help to address their substance use. It is important, if possible, to provide continuity of care—for example, if the client is an inpatient, liaising with the community team concerning the progress that the client has made during BIMI. This process would be facilitated by having a planning meeting with the client and the clinician from the community services team to discuss the work, the client's goals, and strategies to translate gains to a community setting.

◀ **CHAPTER TWO** ▶

Getting Started: Engagement and Brief Assessment

▶ Staying Motivated

To successfully work with a client, and not become discouraged and despondent when he or she initially engages but the next time says "I am not interested," it may be necessary for you to take a step back and perhaps remind yourself of how long it may have taken you to change a "habit" in your own life. There is a need to take into account a number of factors that will influence how BIMI progresses and what is seen as a "successful" result. These include reminding yourself that "ambivalence" is a normal part of the change process, and that change usually occurs over time. Also, the client may not have come into treatment or hospital willingly this time or in the past, and hence may be quite angry about mental health services or being in hospital— and yet, however, may welcome having an opportunity to talk to someone. Therefore, keep an open, non-judgmental, and reflective style; remain optimistic; and take a long-term perspective.

During your initial session with the client, you can use the brief assessment to engage the client in talking openly about drug and alcohol use, mental health, and general well-being. It is

Brief Integrated Motivational Intervention: A Treatment Manual for Co-occurring Mental Health and Substance Use Problems, First Edition. Hermine L. Graham, Alex Copello, Max Birchwood, and Emma Griffith.
© 2016 John Wiley & Sons, Ltd. Published 2016 by John Wiley & Sons, Ltd.
Companion Website: www.wiley.com/go/graham/bimi

possible that he or she has not really had a chance to sit back and talk about the role of alcohol or drug use in poor mental health and/or hospital admissions. During this hospital admission or period, with time on their hands, it may be an opportunity for clients to reflect and develop greater awareness.

> Your aim:
> - Build a good working relationship with the client
> - Increase the client's awareness about the impact of alcohol and drugs
> - Introduce the client to the idea that change is possible

▶ STEP 1: Building Engagement and Assessment

Session Content	Session Goals
STEP 1: Building Engagement and Assessment	
Carry out brief assessment and score questionnaires	■ Engagement and building rapport
Provide personalized feedback to the client from the assessment regarding:	■ Gathering information about the client's use, to build awareness of the impact of substance use
■ Levels of use	■ Building awareness of the impact of substance use on mental health
■ Identify the client's thoughts about the feedback	■ Identifying issues for next session(s)
■ Potential impact of substance use on mental health	
Provide material regarding:	
■ Drug and alcohol use and national patterns/ norms	
■ Impact on mental health, functioning, and relapse	

The assessment completed as part of BIMI is intended to be completed within the context of the broader clinical and risk assessments, and information gathering completed as part of the psychiatric inpatient admission or mental health treatment care plan. The core elements of the brief assessment do not therefore include the completion of a semi-structured clinical interview; instead, they focus in the first session on the completion of questionnaires by the client and, in the second session, the feedback of these results to the client.

▶ Session One Overview

The first session of BIMI is a vital session. This initial meeting represents the first time you and the client will have met specifically for the purpose of *talking openly about alcohol and drug use and building motivation to change substance misuse.* You may have already been working with this client as part of his or her treatment, and so it is important to ensure that BIMI sessions are seen differently and represent "protected" time for you and the client. In the first session of BIMI, when you are completing the relevant questionnaires on the BIMI Brief Assessment Sheet, it is an important opportunity to build a good collaborative working relationship with the client. Following this, the questionnaires are scored, and then personalized feedback developed. The second session then focuses on sharing the *personalized Assessment Feedback Sheet,* called "Your Results," with the client and leaving him or her with a copy of it.

> The initial session aims:
> - To develop a non-judgmental, working relationship where the client feels that he or she can talk openly with you about his or her alcohol and drug use
> - Complete the questionnaires that are relevant to the client and develop personalized assessment feedback

▶ Session One Outline

> Remember, for this session you will need:
> - The BIMI Brief Assessment Sheet to complete with the client

Start by introducing yourself and explaining what BIMI is about. You can use a statement such as the example given in the following text and adapt it according to the setting and client.

- The time people spend in hospital (*or* when they start to feel unwell) can be a time when they think about their lives, including about the use of drugs and alcohol. Our aim is to help support people to do this and to help them explore how drug and alcohol use may have played an important part in their being admitted to a hospital (*or* them feeling unwell).

■ *Why have you been chosen?* We want to invite people who are on inpatient units (*or* are experiencing mental health problems) and who have used alcohol or drugs to have an opportunity to talk.

■ *What will it involve?* We will meet for about three to six brief meetings (each will last about 15–30 minutes). This first meeting will involve some questionnaires about how you are feeling and about drugs and alcohol, and hence may take a little longer. Next time we meet, we will look together at all of this information, and you can talk about how you feel and about your drug and alcohol use. If you start to feel uncomfortable and decide that you no longer want to talk about this, we can stop, and it will not affect the care you receive.

■ Let us start by talking about alcohol and drug use...

At this point, you will need to systematically take the client through the BIMI Brief Assessment Sheet (you can find a copy of it on pages 15–19; all the questionnaires included in it are described in the next section titled "BIMI Brief Assessment" on pages 15–19). This information is designed to be collected from the client *using a conversational style*. Completion of this assessment measure will take approximately 30–40 minutes. It is important that you adopt an open, non-judgmental approach while collecting this information about the client's alcohol and drug use. Remember not to express shock or surprise; your aim is simply to develop a non-judgmental working relationship where the client feels able to talk openly and honestly about his or her alcohol and drug use. If you are not familiar with the drugs the client is using or how he or she uses them, invite him or her to describe the drugs and tell you about them. This will serve to engage the client in a collaborative working relationship with you. If you are certain that the client is using other substances but has not reported it, focus on what he or she is willing to talk about at this stage. The client may feel comfortable to bring it up at a later stage. Remember when you are completing the BIMI Brief Assessment to turn the worksheet to the client, so that he or she can see it and the information is gathered collaboratively. Ensuring the client feels involved in the process will serve to aide engagement and help them recognize their expertise in their own experience.

BIMI Brief Assessment

The questionnaires included in the BIMI Brief Assessment in Session One are fairly short, easy to complete, and based on the substances the client reports using. The structure for the BIMI Brief Assessment is provided in Table 2.1 (pages 15–19). The important areas covered and information on how to score the questionnaires included in the BIMI Brief Assessment are outlined here. These questionnaires are included as they are quick to complete (takes about 30 minutes), easy to use, and readily available.

■ To measure what and how much the client is currently using

A useful questionnaire that can be used here is based on Part B of the *Maudsley Addiction Profile (MAP)* (Marsden et al., 1998). The aim here is to systematically take the client through each substance in turn, asking all the questions about alcohol first before moving to the next substance. This will allow you to build a picture of the client's use of each substance and engage the client in feeling comfortable talking to you about it. When you have finished gathering information about each substance, ask the client to identify which substance is the *main* one he or she uses.

■ To measure the severity of the client's substance use

Alcohol: If the client reported using alcohol, a useful questionnaire to measure the severity and impact of alcohol use is the *Alcohol Use Disorders Identification Test*, commonly referred to as "AUDIT." It is well established and was developed by the World Health Organization (Saunders, Aasland, Babor, Fuente & Grant, 1993). It has 10 questions, with each item scored on a scale of 0–4. Total possible scores range from 0 to 40. A score of 8 or more is suggested to indicate a strong likelihood of "hazardous/harmful" alcohol use. Take the client through each of the 10 questions in turn.

To score it: Add up the scores from each of the 10 questions to give you the total score. Based on the total score:

Did your client score 8 or more?

This is associated with *harmful* or *hazardous drinking*.

Did your client score 13 or more?

Scores of 13 or more in women and 15 or more in men are likely to indicate *alcohol dependence*.

Drugs: If the client reported using drugs, a useful questionnaire to measure the severity and impact of drug use is the *Severity of Dependence Scale* (SDS) (Gossop et al., 1995). It can be used for various drugs and has five questions on a four-point scale that ranges from 0 (never/almost never) to 3 (always/nearly always). Total possible scores range from 0 to 15; a score of 4 or more is suggested to be indicative of *dependency*. If the client identified a drug as his or her *main* substance, take him or her through each of the five questions, inserting the name of the *main* substance.

To score it: Add up the scores from each of the five questions to give you the total score. Based on the total score:

Did your client score 4 or more?

This is said to suggest *dependency*.

■ To measure motivation

A simple way to measure motivation is to use the "Importance–Confidence Ruler." The Importance–Confidence Ruler is a global assessment of the level of motivation and confidence to change, and it assesses two concepts suggested to underpin readiness to change (Rollnick, Butler & Stott, 1997). Using the scale of 0–10, ask the client to (1) rate the importance of making a change to his or her *main* substance use, and to (2) rate how confident he or she feels about making a change in the use of his or her *main* substance.

To score it: Ask your client to rate, on a scale of 0–10, how important it is to change the use of the specified substance, and to rate, on a scale of 0–10, how confident they are that they would succeed. Based on the rating they provide, this roughly indicates his or her perceived level of importance and confidence.

■ To measure mental health

Two useful questionnaires that are quick and freely available to download and measure mental health problems that the client might be experiencing are the nine-item version of the *Patient Health Questionnaire* (PHQ-9) and seven-item version of the

Generalized Anxiety Disorder (GAD-7). They assess depression and anxiety, respectively, and are well established and validated questionnaires (Kroenke, Spitzer & William, 2001; Spitzer, Kroenke, Williams & Löwe, 2006). The measures can be downloaded from: www.phqscreeners.com. Information about them and how to score them can be found at: www.phqscreeners.com/instructions/instructions.pdf.

PHQ-9: To assess the severity of depression, there are nine questions, with the scores for each ranging from 0 (not at all) to 3 (nearly every day).

To score it: The score from each question is added together to give the total score, which can range from 0 to 27.

Did your client score 5?

This represents the cut-off point for *mild depression*.

Did your client score 10?

This represents the cut-off point for *moderate depression*.

Did your client score 15?

This represents the cut-off point for *moderately severe depression*.

Did your client score 20?

This represents the cut-off point for *severe depression*.

GAD-7: To assess the severity of anxiety, there are seven questions, and the scores for each range from 0 (not at all) to 3 (nearly every day).

To score it: The score from each question is added together to give the total score, which can range from 0 to 21.

Did your client score 5?

This represents the cut-off point for *mild anxiety*.

Did your client score 10?

This represents the cut-off point for *moderate anxiety*.

Did your client score 15?

This represents the cut-off point for *severe anxiety*.

Table 2.1 BIMI Brief Assessment Sheet.

	Alcohol	Cannabis	Crack Cocaine	Cocaine Powder	Legal Highs	Heroin	Illicit Methadone	Amphetamine	Other
Have you used this in the past 30 days?									
When did you last use this?									
What is the amount you use on a typical day?									
How much do you spend on this on a typical day?									
What route? Oral Smoke/ Chase Snort/Sniff Intravenous									
During a typical week how frequently would you use this?									
How old were you when you first used this?									
Which substance is the *main* one you use?									

Source: Drug and alcohol use in the past 30 days (based on MAP, Marsden et al., 1998)

AUDIT

Questions	Scoring System					Your Score
	0	1	2	3	4	
1 How often do you have a drink containing alcohol?	Never	Monthly or less	2–4 times per month	2–3 times per week	4+ times per week	
2 How many units of alcohol do you drink on a typical day when you are drinking?	1–2	3–4	5–6	7–8	10+	
3 How often have you had 6 or more units if female, or 8 or more if male, on a single occasion in the last year?	Never	Less than monthly	Monthly	Weekly	Daily or almost daily	
4 How often during the last year have you found that you were not able to stop drinking once you had started?	Never	Less than monthly	Monthly	Weekly	Daily or almost daily	
5 How often during the last year have you failed to do what was normally expected from you because of your drinking?	Never	Less than monthly	Monthly	Weekly	Daily or almost daily	
6 How often during the last year have you needed an alcoholic drink in the morning to get yourself going after a heavy drinking session?	Never	Less than monthly	Monthly	Weekly	Daily or almost daily	
7 How often during the last year have you had a feeling of guilt or remorse after drinking?	Never	Less than monthly	Monthly	Weekly	Daily or almost daily	
8 How often during the last year have you been unable to remember what happened the night before because you had been drinking?	Never	Less than monthly	Monthly	Weekly	Daily or almost daily	
9 Have you or somebody else been injured as a result of your drinking?	No		Yes, but not in the last year		Yes, during the last year	
10 Has a relative or friend, doctor, or other health worker been concerned about your drinking or suggested that you cut down?	No		Yes, but not in the last year		Yes, during the last year	

Source: Saunders et al., 1993

Severity of Dependence Scale (Gossop et al., 1995)

Tell your client: "Please think of your use of _____ during a recent period of using when you answer these questions."

1. Did you think that your use of _____ was out of control?

☐ 0. Never/   ☐ 1. Sometimes   ☐ 2. Often   ☐ 3. Always/
    almost never   nearly always

2. Did the prospect of missing a fix (or dose), make you anxious or worried?

☐ 0. Never/   ☐ 1. Sometimes   ☐ 2. Often   ☐ 3. Always/
    almost never   nearly always

3. Did you worry about your use of _____?

☐ 0. Never/   ☐ 1. Sometimes   ☐ 2. Often   ☐ 3. Always/
    almost never   nearly always

4. Did you wish you could stop?

☐ 0. Never/   ☐ 1. Sometimes   ☐ 2. Often   ☐ 3. Always/
    almost never   nearly always

5. How difficult did you find it to stop or go without _____?

☐ 0. Not difficult   ☐ 1. Quite difficult   ☐ 2. Very difficult   ☐ 3. Impossible

IMPORTANCE–CONFIDENCE RULER

Ask your client: On a scale of 0–10, how important is it right now for you to change your use of _____ [insert name of substance]?

Importance: 0_____10

On a scale of 0–10, if you decide to change, how confident are you that you would succeed?

Confidence: 0 _____ 10

MOOD
PHQ-9

Name <u>Crystal M</u>   Date _____

Over the *last 2 weeks*, how often have you been bothered by any of the following problems?	Not at all	Several days	More than half the days	Nearly every day
1. Little interest or pleasure in doing things	0	1	2	3
2. Feeling down, depressed, or hopeless	0	1	2	3
3. Trouble falling or staying asleep, or sleeping too much	0	1	2	3
4. Feeling tired or having little energy	0	1	2	3
5. Poor appetite or overeating	0	1	2	3
6. Feeling bad about yourself—or that you are a failure or have let yourself or your family down	0	1	2	3
7. Trouble concentrating on things, such as reading the newspaper or watching television	0	1	2	3
8. Moving or speaking so slowly that other people could have noticed? Or the opposite—being so fidgety or restless that you have been moving around a lot more than usual	0	1	2	3
9. Having thoughts that you would be better off dead or of hurting yourself in some way	0	1	2	3

(For office coding: total score _____ = _____ + _____ + _____)

If you checked off *any* problems, how *difficult* have these problems made it for you to do your work, take care of things at home, or get along with other people?

Not difficult at all	Somewhat difficult	Very difficult	Extremely difficult
☐	☐	☐	☐

GAD-7

Over the <u>last 2 weeks</u>, how often have you been bothered by the following problems?	Not at all	Several days	More than half the days	Nearly every day
1. Feeling nervous, anxious or on edge	0	1	2	3
2. Not being able to stop or control worrying	0	1	2	3
3. Worrying too much about different things	0	1	2	3
4. Trouble relaxing	0	1	2	3
5. Being so restless that it is hard to sit still	0	1	2	3
6. Becoming easily annoyed or irritable	0	1	2	3
7. Feeling afraid as if something awful might happen	0	1	2	3

Total Score ___ = Add Columns ___ + ___ + ___

If you checked off <u>any</u> problems, how <u>difficult</u> have these problems made it for you to do your work, take care of things at home, or get along with other people?

Not difficult at all	Somewhat difficult	Very difficult	Extremely difficult
☐	☐	☐	☐

The PHQ-9 and GAD-7 questionnaires have been developed by Drs. Robert L. Spitzer, Janet B. W. Williams, Kurt Kroenke, and colleagues, with an educational grant from Pfizer Inc. No permission required to reproduce, translate, display, or distribute.

Using the illustrative case examples of Sam, Sebastian, and Crystal, you will gain a sense of how to take clients through the *BIMI Brief Assessment* (see pages 26–28, Table 2.2 for their completed assessments).

Case example: Sam

Sam is a 33-year-old man who has been admitted to an acute mental health inpatient ward for the past 2 weeks. He has been diagnosed as experiencing schizophrenia for the past 10 years. He has been detained in hospital for assessment and treatment as he was becoming increasingly anxious and paranoid and could not keep himself safe prior to being admitted. He had also stopped taking his medication, as he worries that it makes him put on a lot of weight and he does not believe it helps him. He has been quite withdrawn and depressed in mood since coming to the hospital. Sam has said that, before coming to the hospital, smoking cannabis was the only thing that interested him, and that he has smoked it since he was 15 years of age.

- So Sam, if we think about the past month, and particularly the weeks just before you came into hospital, "have you used *alcohol* in the past 30 days?"

As Sam has reported no alcohol use, you would need to move onto the next substance listed in the BIMI Brief Assessment, which is cannabis.

- So Sam, if we think about the past month, and particularly the weeks just before you came into hospital, "have you used *cannabis* in the past 30 days?"
- "Can you remember when you last used?"
- Thinking about your use in general, "What is the amount you use on a typical day?"
- And "How much do you spend on a typical day?"
- "How do you usually take *cannabis*?"
- And "During a typical week how frequently would you use *cannabis*?"
- Thinking about how long you have used, "How old were you when you first used *cannabis*?"
- And "Is this *cannabis* the main substance you use?"

You would then need to ask the client if he or she has used any of the other drugs. Go through asking if he or she has used each drug in turn, as it may be that the client initially may say he or she is only using one substance but as the client begins to relax and engage with you during the assessment he or she may feel more able to be open about other substances used. So, using the case of Sam, you would ask:

- So Sam, if we think about the past month, and particularly the weeks just before you came into hospital, "Have you used *crack cocaine* in the past 30 days?"

Sam reports no *crack cocaine* use in the past 30 days, so you move onto asking about the next substance.

■ So Sam, if we think about the past month, and particularly the weeks just before you came into hospital, "Have you used *cocaine powder* in the past 30 days?"

Sam reports no *cocaine powder* use in the past 30 days, so you move onto asking about the next substance.

■ So Sam, if we think about the past month, and particularly the weeks just before you came into hospital, "Have you used *legal highs* in the past 30 days?"

Sam reports no *legal high* use in the past 30 days, so you move onto asking about the next substance.

■ So Sam, if we think about the past month, and particularly the weeks just before you came into hospital, "Have you used *heroin* in the past 30 days?"

Sam reports no *heroin* use in the past 30 days, so you move onto asking about the next substance.

■ So Sam, if we think about the past month, and particularly the weeks just before you came into hospital, "Have you used *illicit methadone* in the past 30 days?"

Sam reports no *illicit methadone* use in the past 30 days, so you move onto asking about the next substance.

■ So Sam, if we think about the past month, and particularly the weeks just before you came into hospital, "Have you used *amphetamine* in the past 30 days?"

Sam reports no *amphetamine* use in the past 30 days, so you move onto asking about the next substance.

■ So Sam, if we think about the past month, and particularly the weeks just before you came into hospital, "Have you used *any other substance/drug* in the past 30 days?"

Sam reports no *other substance/drug* use in the past 30 days, so you move onto the next questionnaire.

You will now need to complete either the AUDIT or SDS questionnaire with the client, depending on what the client reports as the substance that he or she uses. If the client reports that he or she uses *alcohol*, then you complete AUDIT; if the client reports that he or she uses drugs, you will need to complete *SDS* next. For SDS, insert the name of the main drug the client reports using in the assessment worksheet. So, in the case of Sam, he reports that *cannabis* is the main substance he uses, so SDS is completed for cannabis. Remember to turn the BIMI Brief Assessment worksheet to the client, so that he or she can see it.

- Thank you Sam, for starting to talk with me about the substance(s) you have used. Thinking a bit more about your use of cannabis ... "Please think of your use of cannabis during a recent period of using when you answer these questions." Answer using one of the responses listed here: "never/almost never"; "sometimes"; "often"; and "always/nearly always."

- So, thinking about a recent period of using, "did you think that your use of cannabis was out of control?"

- And "did the prospect of missing a fix make you feel anxious or worried?"

- At that time, "did you worry about your use of cannabis?"

- And "did you wish you could stop?" Leading on from this, "how difficult did you find it to stop or go without cannabis?"

- Thank you for answering these questions Sam, we have three more to complete, and the next one has just two questions.

- The first question is, "On a scale of 0–10, how important is it right now for you to change your use of cannabis?"

- And, should you decide to make a change, on a scale of 0–10, if you decide to change, how confident are you that you would succeed?

- The final area that would be important for us to think about are how you have been feeling over the past 2 weeks. Similar to the questionnaire we did earlier, there are responses to use when you are answering these questions; please have a look at these responses and choose one that best fits with how you have been feeling. *So,* "Over the *last 2 weeks*, how often have you been bothered by any of the following problems?"

- The first one is "Little interest or pleasure in doing things" and the next "Feeling down, depressed, or hopeless."
- In the last 2 weeks, have you had "Trouble falling or staying asleep, or sleeping too much," or with "Feeling tired or having little energy"?
- Have you, found over the last 2 weeks you have experienced "Poor appetite or overeating" or found that you were "Feeling bad about yourself" or that "you are a failure or have let yourself or your family down?"
- Did you have "Trouble concentrating on things, such as reading the newspaper or watching television," or were you "Moving or speaking so slowly that other people could have noticed"? Or the opposite—"Being so fidgety or restless that you have been moving around a lot more than usual"?
- Finally, during the last 2 weeks, have you had "Thoughts that you would be better off dead or of hurting yourself in some way"?

It would be essential, if the client reported any risk or endorsed question nine on the PHQ-9, that a full risk assessment and risk management plan be implemented in line with your service guidelines.

If the client indicates that he or she experienced any problems on the PHQ-9 questionnaire, then you will need to ask him or her to answer an additional question.

- "If you checked off *any* problems," we then need to think about "how *difficult* have these problems made it for you to do your work, take care of things at home, or get along with other people?"
- Using the responses here (i.e., "not difficult at all"; "Somewhat difficult"; "very difficult"; and "extremely difficult"), which one represents how you feel?
- We are now on the last questionnaire. This one is quite similar to the one we have just done in the way it is set out, so I would like you to again think "over the past 2 weeks, how often have you been bothered by the following problems?" Use the responses written here to reply.
- So, over the last 2 weeks, have you been "feeling nervous, anxious, or on edge"?

- or found yourself "not being able to stop or control worrying"
- Did you find you were "worrying too much about different things"
- Did you have "trouble relaxing"
- Did you find yourself "being so restless that it is hard to sit still"
- Over the last 2 weeks, did you find you were "becoming easily annoyed or irritable" or "feeling afraid as if something awful might happen"
- Finally, as we did for the last questionnaire: "if you have checked off any problem, how difficult have these problems made it for you to do your work, take care of things at home, or get along with other people" Let's use the rating scale shown to think about this.

Case example: Sebastian

Sebastian is a 49-year-old man who has described feeling anxious and very low in mood, and is being seen at home by community mental health services. He describes finding it difficult to leave his house because of these problems over the past 2 weeks. He has been diagnosed as experiencing bipolar affective disorder since he was 28 years of age. He usually takes his medication regularly but sometimes forgets. There are a number of empty alcohol cans around his home, and he regularly smells of alcohol.

Using the illustrative case example of Sebastian, the BIMI Brief Assessment would be completed in the same way with Sebastian as it was with Sam; however, Sebastian only reports *alcohol* use, and, since this is his main substance, you would complete AUDIT, which focuses on his use of alcohol, *rather than* completing SDS. To complete AUDIT, you would read the statements exactly and record Sebastian's answers. Begin AUDIT by saying:

- "Now I am going to ask you some questions about your use of alcoholic beverages during this past year."

Explain what is meant by "alcoholic beverages" by using local examples of beer, wine, vodka, etc., and then carry on through each of the AUDIT questions. For example:

- So Sebastian, thinking about your use of *alcohol*; "Now I am going to ask you some questions about your use of alcoholic beverages during this past year"; when I say alcoholic beverages I mean, for example, "beer, wine, or vodka." The instructions for this questionnaire say I need to read these questions exactly, so here we go.

You would then proceed with completing the remaining questionnaires in the BIMI Brief Assessment—that is, the *Importance–Confidence Ruler; PHQ-9;* and *GAD-7*—as outlined in the case of Sam.

Case example: Crystal

Crystal is a 27-year-old woman who has been admitted to an acute mental health inpatient ward for the past 2 weeks. She has been diagnosed as experiencing paranoid psychosis. She voluntarily agreed to stay in hospital for assessment and treatment as she was becoming increasingly anxious and paranoid prior to being admitted. Crystal has said that she drinks alcohol and smokes cannabis. You are also aware, from the information recorded in her case notes, that she uses crack cocaine, but she does not initially report this to you.

Using the illustrative case example of Crystal, you would complete the BIMI Brief Assessment with Crystal in the same way as you would with both Sam and Sebastian, as outlined in the preceding text. Starting with the MAP, you would go through asking her if she has used each substance listed *in turn.* As you go through this with Crystal, she initially reports that she is only using *alcohol* and *cannabis.* At this stage, Crystal reports no crack cocaine use. In this case, it would be important to carry on with asking about the other substances in a non-judgmental manner, without telling her that you know from her clinical notes that she has used crack cocaine. It may be the case that the client may report this at a later stage when he or she feels ready to. In this case scenario, as Crystal begins to relax and engage, you notice that she starts to become more open about her substance use and mentions that she has used crack cocaine in the past. At this stage, you would ask:

- So Crystal, if we think about the past month, and particularly the weeks just before you came into hospital, "have you used crack cocaine in the past 30 days?"

This invites Crystal to revisit the question concerning crack cocaine at a different stage in the meeting. In the case example, Crystal reports her crack cocaine use, and says it is the main substance she uses. This information is then recorded, and both the SDS and AUDIT questionnaires are completed as Crystal reports she is using both drugs and alcohol. When working with Crystal as a poly-substance user, it is important to be specific when completing SDS about which substance is being considered. This would be completed for the *main* substance, since this will be the focus of the information within the assessment feedback. The remaining questionnaires on the BIMI Brief Assessment Sheet would then be completed as outlined in the cases of Sam and Sebastian.

Table 2.2 BIMI Brief Assessment—*Case Example Crystal.*

	Alcohol	Cannabis	Crack Cocaine	Cocaine Powder	Legal Highs	Heroin	Illicit Methadone	Amphetamine	Other
Have you used this in the past 30 days?	Yes	Yes	Yes	No	No	No	No	No	No
When did you last use this?	2 weeks ago	2 weeks ago	2 weeks ago						
What is the amount you use on a typical day?	Two cans	About two spliffs	Not every day (£55 each time)						
How much do you spend on this on a typical day?	£2	I spend about £1.25 (£10 per week)	About £55 each time						
What route? Oral Smoke/Chase Snort/Sniff Intravenous	Oral	Smoke	Smoke						
During a typical week, how frequently would you use this?	3 days a week	Every day	About 2 times						
How old were you when you first used this?	13 years old	15 years old	25 years old						
Which substance is the *main* one you use?			Crack						

Source: Drug and alcohol use in the past 30 days (based on MAP, Marsden et al., 1998)

AUDIT

Questions	Scoring System					Your Score
	0	1	2	3	4	
1 How often do you have a drink containing alcohol?	Never	Monthly or less	2–4 times per month	2–3 times per week	4+ times per week	3
2 How many units of alcohol do you drink on a typical day when you are drinking?	1–2	3–4	5–6	7–8	10+	1
3 How often have you had six or more units if female, or eight or more if male, on a single occasion in the last year?	Never	Less than monthly	Monthly	Weekly	Daily or almost daily	1
4 How often during the last year have you found that you were not able to stop drinking once you had started?	Never	Less than monthly	Monthly	Weekly	Daily or almost daily	1
5 How often during the last year have you failed to do what was normally expected from you because of your drinking?	Never	Less than monthly	Monthly	Weekly	Daily or almost daily	0
6 How often during the last year have you needed an alcoholic drink in the morning to get yourself going after a heavy drinking session?	Never	Less than monthly	Monthly	Weekly	Daily or almost daily	0
7 How often during the last year have you had a feeling of guilt or remorse after drinking?	Never	Less than monthly	Monthly	Weekly	Daily or almost daily	0
8 How often during the last year have you been unable to remember what happened the night before because you had been drinking?	Never	Less than monthly	Monthly	Weekly	Daily or almost daily	0
9 Have you or somebody else been injured as a result of your drinking?	No		Yes, but not in the last year		Yes, during the last year	0
10 Has a relative or friend, doctor, or other health worker been concerned about your drinking or suggested that you cut down?	No		Yes, but not in the last year		Yes, during the last year	0

Source: Saunders et al., 1993

SDS

Tell your client: "Please think of your use of <u>CRACK</u> during a recent period of using when you answer these questions."

1. Did you think that your use of <u>CRACK</u> was out of control?

☐ 0. Never/ almost never ☐ 1. Sometimes ☐ **2. Often** ☐ 3. Always/ nearly always

2. Did the prospect of missing a fix (or dose), make you anxious or worried?

☐ 0. Never/ almost never ☐ 1. Sometimes ☐ **2. Often** ☐ 3. Always/ nearly always

3. Did you worry about your use of <u>CRACK</u>?

☐ 0. Never/ almost never ☐ **1. Sometimes** ☐ 2. Often ☐ 3. Always/ nearly always

4. Did you wish you could stop?

☐ 0. Never/ almost never ☐ **1. Sometimes** ☐ 2. Often ☐ 3. Always/ nearly always

5. How difficult did you find it to stop or go without <u>CRACK</u>?

☐ 0. Not difficult ☐ **1. Quite difficult** ☐ 2. Very difficult ☐ 3. Impossible

Source: Gossop et al., 1995

IMPORTANCE–CONFIDENCE RULER

Ask your client: On a scale of 0–10, how important is it right now for you to change your use of _____ [insert name of substance]?

Importance: 0_____5_____10

On a scale of 0–10, if you decide to change, how confident are you that you would succeed?

Confidence: 0_____2_____10

MOOD
PHQ-9

Name <u>Crystal M</u>   Date _____

Over the *last 2 weeks*, how often have you been bothered by any of the following problems?	Not at all	Several days	More than half the days	Nearly every day
1. Little interest or pleasure in doing things	0	1	2	**3**
2. Feeling down, depressed, or hopeless	0	1	2	**3**
3. Trouble falling or staying asleep, or sleeping too much	0	1	**2**	3
4. Feeling tired or having little energy	0	1	2	**3**
5. Poor appetite or overeating	0	**1**	2	3
6. Feeling bad about yourself—or that you are a failure or have let yourself or your family down	0	1	**2**	3
7. Trouble concentrating on things, such as reading the newspaper or watching television	0	**1**	2	3
8. Moving or speaking so slowly that other people could have noticed? Or the opposite—being so fidgety or restless that you have been moving around a lot more than usual	0	**1**	2	3
9. Thoughts that you would be better off dead or of hurting yourself in some way	**0**	1	2	3

(For office coding: total score <u>**15**</u> = <u>**4**</u> + <u>**2**</u> + <u>**9**</u>)

If you checked off *any* problems, how *difficult* have these problems made it for you to do your work, take care of things at home, or get along with other people?

Not difficult at all	Somewhat difficult	*Very difficult*	Extremely difficult
☐	☐	☐	☐

GAD-7

Over the last 2 weeks, how often have you been bothered by the following problems?	Not at all	Several days	More than half the days	Nearly every day
1. Feeling nervous, anxious or on edge	0	1	2	3
2. Not being able to stop or control worrying	0	1	2	3
3. Worrying too much about different things	0	1	2	3
4. Trouble relaxing	0	1	2	3
5. Being so restless that it is hard to sit still	0	1	2	3
6. Becoming easily annoyed or irritable	0	1	2	3
7. Feeling afraid as if something awful might happen	0	1	2	3

Total Score ___ = Add Columns ___ + ___ + ___

If you checked off any problems, how difficult have these problems made it for you to do your work, take care of things at home, or get along with other people?

Not difficult at all	Somewhat difficult	Very difficult	Extremely difficult
☐	☐	☐	☐

Crystal's score: TOTAL SCORE = 1 + 6 + 12 = 19

During and after completing the BIMI Brief Assessment, it is important to encourage the client to keep going and acknowledge that the client has worked hard to do this. It may help to remind the client that the information he or she provides will be very helpful, as the results of the assessment will be fed back to him or her the next time you meet. Once you have completed the BIMI Brief Assessment, encourage the client to reflect on the topics covered and how they feel, for example, as shown in the following text.

- Today, we have talked about your substance use and about how you have been feeling, and we have completed a few questionnaires. What did you think about the questionnaires and what they covered?
- Were you surprised by any of the questions? If so, why?

- How have you felt about spending time thinking about you use of _____ [insert substance]?
- How are you feeling after having completed the questionnaires?
- Do you have any questions?
- When we meet the next time, I shall give you some feedback on "Your Results," and we can think about any questions that you might have and information that you might find useful.
- Let us make time to meet again.

At the end of Session One, you will need to finalize the date for the next session with the client.

So, remember:

- When completing the BIMI Brief Assessment with your client, it is important to focus both on engaging the client in the process and on following the guidelines for the completion of the questionnaires (i.e., using the exact wording) on the BIMI Brief Assessment Sheet.

- After completing the BIMI Brief Assessment Sheet, spend time discussing with your client how they found this process and how they are feeling.

- Ensure your client knows that, having invested time in completing the questionnaires, you will discuss the result with him or her the next time you meet.

- If the client reports any risk or endorses question 9 of the PHQ-9, ensure that a full risk assessment and risk management plan be implemented in line with your service guidelines.

Generating the Personalized Assessment Feedback Sheet

Once you have completed Session One and the questionnaires with the client, score the questionnaires according to the scoring guidelines detailed in the BIMI Brief Assessment section (pages 15–19), and then insert these details into the relevant sections of the assessment feedback sheet template provided (see Table 2.1, pages 15–19). The illustrative case examples of Sam, Sebastian, and Crystal (given in Table 2.2) illustrate how this can be done.

Assessment Feedback Sheet, part 1

In this section, insert the relevant information, obtained from completing the MAP (part B), for each substance used. Indicate in this section how much the client is using per day. For alcohol use, you can include here the units of alcohol. If the client is using alcohol, you will need to work out how many units this equates to by using a units calculator. The units and calories calculator on the Drinkaware website is easy and straightforward to use (www. drinkaware.co.uk/tips-and-tools/drink-diary). In the "Amount spent" box, include how much money the client's drug and/or alcohol use equates to per week. If the client reports that he or she is not currently using a particular substance, you can indicate this by including the term "not used." For alcohol users, you will note that the current "Lower risk guidelines" are already included in the template. There is a box in this section to include the score obtained from AUDIT for alcohol use, and SDS for drug use.

Assessment Feedback Sheet, part 2

In this section, alcohol and drug use is explained in words and compared to rates of use in the general population. Information from the measures of mental health and motivation to change are also included. The final section in part 2 of the Assessment Feedback Sheet includes information about the impact of alcohol or drugs on mental health.

ALCOHOL OR DRUG USE

The standard statement included in the provided template that you will need to personalize is:

"You said you were using _____ [insert quantity used and frequency of use], which cost about _____ [insert financial cost]. When we have a look at the drug/alcohol use across the country for adults, _____ [insert relevant information related to prevalence for relevant country in the general population]. The research suggests that about _____ [e.g., insert general population percentage] use more than once a month."

You then invite the client to reflect on this and discuss it by including statements such as: "What do you make of that information? Is it what you expected, or different from what you expected?"

Following this, a description of what the AUDIT or SDS scores mean, from the scoring guidelines, is included (e.g., in the case of Sebastian, an AUDIT score of 10 equates to the following description: "Your results suggested that your use of alcohol is at a level that is often associated with 'harmful or hazardous' drinking"):

"Your results suggested that your use of _____ [insert name of substance] is at a level that is often associated with _____ [insert information concerning level of use from AUDIT/SDS]."

You then invite the patient to reflect on this and discuss it by including statements such as:

"What do you make of this result?"

MOTIVATION TO CHANGE

The standard statement included in the provided template that you will need to personalize is:

"Your results suggest that you felt it was _____ [insert statement based on the rating on the importance scale], but also felt that you were _____ [insert statement based on the rating on the confidence scale] confident that you could make a change in your _____ [insert name of substance] used if you decided you wanted to."

You then invite the patient to reflect on this and discuss it by including a statement such as:

"Is this still the case?"

YOUR MOOD

The standard statement included in the provided template, that you will need to personalize is:

"Your scores suggested that, at that time, you were feeling _____ [insert statement from anxiety scores] and _____ [insert statement from depression scores] in mood."

WHAT RESEARCH SUGGESTS ABOUT THE IMPACT OF _____ [insert name of substance] USE ON MENTAL HEALTH

The standard statement included in the provided template that you will need to personalize is:

"One of the leaflets from _____ [insert name of the website—e.g., Talk to Frank or Drinkaware] says that _____ [insert relevant information about the effect of that substance on mental health)."

It is vital, in this final section of part 2 of the Assessment Feedback Sheet, that some information be provided concerning what the current evidence suggests about the impact of the substance being used on mental health. This allows the relationship between mental health and substance use to be explored in light of the client's personalized information. In the illustrative case examples, you can see how this can be done. It is important when drawing together this information that you use recognized and reliable websites to obtain this to gather it and that the information be up to date and relevant. The websites used to obtain the information in the case examples above were Talk to Frank (www.talktofrank.com) and Drinkaware (www.drinkaware.co.uk).

YOUR RESULTS

Diagnosis: _____ Substance of choice: _____

Part 1

ALCOHOL

Alcohol	Your current use	United Kingdom (%)	Lower risk guideline
Per day			Females: 2–3 Males: 3–4
Per week			
Amount spent (£)			
AUDIT score			

DRUGS

Drug	Your current use (per week)	Amount spent (£) (per week)
Cannabis		
Crack/ cocaine		
Ecstasy		
Heroin		
Other		
Total spent (£)		
Dependence score		

Impact of alcohol at current pattern of use:

Part 2

_____ [insert name of substance] USE: You said you were using _____ [insert quantity used and frequency of use], which costs about _____ [insert financial cost]. When we have a look at the drug/alcohol use across the country for adults, _____ [insert relevant information related to prevalence for relevant country in the general population]. The research suggests that about [e.g., insert general population percentage] _____ use more than once a month.

What do you make of that information? Is it what you expected, or different from what you expected?

Your results suggested that your use of _____ [insert name of substance] is at a level that is often associated with _____ [insert information concerning level of use from AUDIT/SDS].

What do you make of this result?

MOTIVATION TO CHANGE: Your results suggest that you felt it was _____ [insert statement based on the rating on the importance scale], but also felt that you were _____ [insert statement based on the rating on the confidence scale] confident that you could make a change in your _____ [insert name of substance] if you decided you wanted to.
Is this still the case?

YOUR MOOD: Your scores suggested that, at that time, you were feeling _____ [insert statement from anxiety scores] and _____ [insert statement from depression scores] in mood.

WHAT RESEARCH SUGGESTS ABOUT THE IMPACT OF _____ [insert name of substance] ON MENTAL HEALTH
One of the leaflets from the _____ [insert name of the website—i.e., Talk to Frank or Drinkaware] says that _____ [insert relevant information for the substance].
We could look at information related to this together next time we meet; what do you think?
For more information, you can look on the website _____ [insert name of the website—i.e., Talk to Frank or Drinkaware].

► Session Two Overview

You start this process by providing the client with feedback from the questionnaires you completed with him or her in the first session, in an open, non-judgmental way. The feedback is presented in the Assessment Feedback Sheet, called "Your Results" (see illustrative examples in Figure 2.1), and this allows the client to think about his or her use in relation to how other people across the country use and to think about the impact of his or her use.

The client will probably have many questions about the feedback, and so responses to some of these questions are provided in the clients' Assessment Feedback Sheet. Further information can be found in psychoeducational leaflets, and in the "Frequently Asked Questions" section on page 42. It would be useful if the client is encouraged to read some tailored psychoeducational information that you will provide and/or access Internet resources to help answer any questions they may have after Session Two. A list of some useful websites is included on page 52).

► Session Two Outline

> Remember, for this session you will need:
>
> - The "Your Results" Assessment Feedback Sheet completed with the client's information
> - Some leaflets or psychoeducational information specifically related to the client's substance use and mental health problems

Session Two initially focuses on discussing with the clients his or her results from the BIMI Brief Assessment. You can start this process by asking the client what he or she thought about the assessment:

- When we first met, we completed a few questionnaires. What did you think about the questionnaires and what they covered?

- Based on the answers you gave when you completed the questionnaires, the results suggest that _____.

Take the client through each section of the client's Assessment Feedback Sheet ("Your Results"). At the end of each section, ask the client what his or her thoughts are to encourage the client to reflect on the content and to personally connect with the information. This will help to build awareness of the impact of substance use, and its impact on mental health.

- How do these results fit with how you feel? Is that how you are feeling still?
- Are there any questions you have? Is there any further information you would like?
- I have brought along some leaflets that I thought you might find helpful. There are also some websites on the Internet that you can look at, if you would like to find more information.
- When we meet next time _____ [give date of next session], we can talk about what you enjoy about using _____ or what keeps you using _____ [insert name of substance].

YOUR RESULTS: *Sam*

Diagnosis: *Schizophrenia* Substance of choice: *Cannabis (skunk)*

Part 1
ALCOHOL

Alcohol	Your current use	United Kingdom (%)	Lower risk guidelines
Per day	None		
Per week			
Amount spent (£)			
AUDIT score			

Impact of alcohol at current pattern of use:
Not used

DRUGS

Drug	Your current use (per week)	Amount spent (£) (per week)
Cannabis	2/8	£70
Crack/ cocaine		
Ecstasy		
Heroin		
Other		
Total spent (£)	70 (per week)	
Dependence score	3	

Part 2

CANNABIS USE: You said you were using about an ounce of skunk a month, which would roughly cost about £280. When we have a look at the drug use across England and Wales (2012–2013) for adults during the previous 12 months, just over 8% had used an illicit drug. Cannabis was the illicit drug most frequently used during the past 12 months, which had been used by under 7% of adults (Home Office, 2013). This report suggests that, when just looking at young adults (age 16–24 years), about 13% had used cannabis during the previous 12 months (Home Office, 2013). What do you make of that information? Is it what you expected, or different from what you expected?

Based on what you said, the results suggest that, due to the level of your use, you could be experiencing some problems related to smoking skunk. Does this fit with what you experience on a daily basis?

MOTIVATION TO CHANGE: Your results suggest that you felt it was very important to change (rating 10), the highest point of the scale, but also felt you were not confident that you could make a change in your skunk use if you decided you wanted to (rating 0).

Your results suggest that you were not dependent on skunk, but that it could be causing you some problems. Does that fit with how you feel now?

YOUR VIEW OF YOUR MENTAL HEALTH/MOOD: Your scores suggest that, at that time, you were feeling a bit anxious and really low in mood. This perhaps reflects what you said at the start of our meeting today.

WHAT RESEARCH SUGGESTS ABOUT THE IMPACT OF CANNABIS ON MENTAL HEALTH

One of the Frank (2011) website says that using cannabis "regularly and for a long time" can lead to a greater risk of experiencing anxiety, depression, and paranoia, and put you at risk of experiencing "psychotic symptoms" and of developing mental health problems—for example, schizophrenia. The leaflet says that, for people who already experience mental health problems, cannabis might cause a relapse of symptoms. It suggests that regular use of cannabis "for a long time" can make it difficult for you to concentrate, that you can lose your motivation, and that it can also affect your physical health. Would you like to know more about the impact on your physical health? To sum up, the leaflet suggests that the biggest risks from cannabis seem to be related to using it "regularly and for a long time," and that these risks could be greater if you are "young, you smoke a lot and you smoke strong cannabis, like skunk."

We could look together at information related to this the next time we meet. What do you think? For more information, you can look on the website (www.talktofrank.com).

YOUR RESULTS: *Sebastian*

Diagnosis: *Bipolar affective disorder*   Substance of choice: *Alcohol*

Part 1

ALCOHOL

Alcohol	Your current use	Lower risk guidelines
Per day	12 units	Males: 3–4
Per week	84 units	
Amount spent (£)	35	
AUDIT score	10	

DRUG

Drug	Your current use (per week)	Amount spent (£) (per week)
Cannabis	None	
Crack/ cocaine	None	
Ecstasy	None	
Heroin	None	
Other	None	
Total spent (£)	None	
Dependence score		

Part 2

ALCOHOL USE: You said that you were using about six cans of 4% lager a day, costing £5, which means if you drank this amount over a week you would have drunk about 42 cans of lager and spend about £35. When we look at this as units of alcohol, this converts to 12 units a day and about 84 units a week.

Do you know what a unit of alcohol is? Shall we look at some information about this first? If we look at the preceding table, we can see the government "lower risk guidelines" for alcohol in units. Drinkaware outline the current UK government lower risk guidelines for men as not regularly having over 3–4 units of alcohol a day; women are recommended to have no more than 2–3 units of alcohol a day regularly (Drinkaware, 2015a). When we look at the numbers of people in the country using alcohol, in England about a quarter of men said "in an average week" they drank over 21 units, and less than a quarter of women described drinking over 14 units "in an average week." The average number of units they were having in a week was about 16 units for men and eight units for women. A big study in America found that about a third of people who had experienced schizophrenia had used alcohol and gotten into some problems with it in their life time.

In the United Kingdom, the NHS describes "binge drinking" as having eight or more units of alcohol in a single session for men and six or more units for women. However, this definition may not apply to everyone as people vary. Would you like to know more about different patterns of alcohol use? Binge drinking usually involves drinking a large quantity of alcohol in a short space of time, or drinking with the end result of becoming drunk. What do you make of this? We can find out more about units by looking at the Drinkaware website (www.drinkaware.co.uk).

Your results suggest that your use of alcohol is at a level that is often associated with "harmful or hazardous" drinking. What do you make of this result?

MOTIVATION TO CHANGE: Your results suggest that you felt it was not important at the moment for you to change your use of alcohol (rating 1 on the scale of 0–10 for importance). However, if you decided to make a change, you felt very confident that you could achieve this (rating this 10/10).

YOUR VIEW OF YOUR MENTAL HEALTH/MOOD: Your scores suggested that, at that time, you were feeling really anxious and really depressed. How does this fit with how you are feeling now?

WHAT RESEARCH SUGGESTS ABOUT THE IMPACT OF ALCOHOL ON YOUR MENTAL HEALTH

The Talk to Frank (2013a) website (www.talktofrank.com/drug/alcohol) says that "Alcohol is a depressant," which means it "slows down your body's responses" in lots of different ways; and also that "way too much alcohol in a single session could put you in a coma or even kill you." The information indicates that drinking alcohol has risks, and the "risks are higher if you drink excessively in a single occasion or drink higher amounts regularly over time." They say if you exceed the lower risk limits "persistently over time," alcohol can cause problems with your physical health, such as cancers, heart disease, and damage to your liver. We can look at more information about the risk of using alcohol for your physical health. Would you like this? Another source of information about alcohol, called Drinkaware (2015; www.drinkaware.co.uk/check-the-facts/health-effects-of-alcohol/mental-health/alcohol-and-mental-health), says that, when you drink heavily, "anxiety and depression are more common." What do you make of this? Would you like to know more about the risk of using alcohol for your mental health?

Would you like us to have a look at some information about binge drinking, which I mentioned earlier?

YOUR RESULTS: *Crystal*

Diagnosis: *Paranoid psychosis*　　　　　Substance of choice: *Crack cocaine*

Part 1
ALCOHOL

Alcohol	Your current use	Lower risk guidelines
Per day	4	Women: 2–3 units
Per week	12	
Amount spent (£)	12	
AUDIT score	4	

DRUGS

Drug	Your current use (per week)	Amount spent (£) (per week)
Cannabis	£10	
Crack/cocaine	£110	
Ecstasy		
Heroin		
Other		
Total spent (£)	130	
Dependence score	8	

Part 2

CRACK USE: You said that you were using about two-tenths (an ⅛th) of crack cocaine a week, which you were smoking using a homemade pipe 3 days a week. Based on what you said you were spending, it would roughly cost you about £140 a week, or £560 a month. When we have a look at the number of people in the country, for adults asked, only about 3% had used a class A drug during the past year, and fewer in the past month. For crack cocaine, it is suggested that only about 0.1% of adults had used this drug during the past month. What do you make of that information?

Your results suggest that your use could be contributing to you experiencing some problems related to smoking crack. How does this fit with what you experience?

MOTIVATION TO CHANGE: You felt that it was perhaps important to change, rating 5, which is the middle point of the scale, but you were not really confident that you could make a change in your crack use if you decided you wanted to (rating 2).

YOUR VIEW OF YOUR MENTAL HEALTH/MOOD: Your scores suggested that you were feeling really anxious at that time and that your mood was a bit low. Does this perhaps reflect what you said at the start of our meeting today?

WHAT RESEARCH SUGGESTS ABOUT THE IMPACT OF CRACK ON MENTAL HEALTH

Information on the Talk to Frank (2013b) website (www.talktofrank.com/drug/cocaine#aka=Crack) describes crack cocaine as a "powerful stimulant" with "short-lived effects." They outline that crack can affect both your mental and physical health—for example, it says "regularly smoking crack can cause breathing problems and pains in the chest." The Talk to Frank website says that "using cocaine a lot makes people feel depressed and run down, and that it can sometimes lead to serious problems with anxiety, paranoia and panic attacks." Importantly, the information indicates that you can die from an overdose, and this risk increases if cocaine is "mixed with other drugs or alcohol." Did you know that using alcohol and cocaine together "can be particularly dangerous, as they mix together in the body to produce a toxic chemical called cocaethylene." Would you like to know more about this? There are other risks associated with using crack—for example, debts from using—that we can talk about if you would like.

We can look at more information together if you would like. What do you think?

▶ Frequently Asked Questions (FAQs)

> Your aim:
> - To build the client's awareness about the impact of substance use
> - Provide an important initial opportunity to help explore the client's concerns, thoughts, and beliefs about substance use and mental health problems
> - To provide the client with relevant, up-to-date information from a reliable source
> - To invite the client to comment and reflect on the information provided throughout the process

By now, you will have met with the client for Session One and be preparing to provide the assessment feedback in Session Two. You will have been focusing on developing a rapport with your client and an environment in which substance use can be discussed openly. It is possible that the client may begin to ask any questions they have concerning their experience of both mental health problems and use of substances as you feed back the results to him or her. These may be questions that the client has had for a long time and not shared with anyone, so prioritizing time to explore and discuss these is important. This provides a good opportunity to provide psychoeducation about the risks associated with the client's drug and/or alcohol use, and the relationship between substance use and mental health. This will build on the information you provided in the Assessment Feedback Sheet.

Some examples of FAQs are provided. These represent suggestions of what may be useful to draw on from the current literature that will help answer these questions. You will need to decide what is appropriate to share with the client at this time, bearing in mind the client's current mental state. This information just provides an introduction; you will probably find that you need specific information for each client, as well as the country and setting you are working in (e.g., concerning the risks to physical or mental health). Every effort has been made to provide relevant and accurate information in our illustrative example answers at the time of preparing the manual. However, when working with your client, it is important to refer to information that is relevant to your client, setting, treatment needs, and country. It is important to note that any information given to a client should be accurate, up-to-date, and from a reliable source. Some suggestions of websites that you might find useful to obtain further information are provided in the following sections.

Alcohol

How much is OK to drink and what is a unit of alcohol?

- Drinkaware outlines the current UK government "lower risk guidelines" for men as not regularly having over *3–4 units* of alcohol a day. Women are recommended to have no more than *2–3 units* of alcohol a day regularly (Drinkaware, 2015a). We can find out more about this by looking at this page on the Drinkaware website: www.drinkaware.co.uk/check-the-facts/what-is-alcohol/daily-guidelines.

- "Regularly" is said to mean "every day or most days of the week" (Drinkaware, 2015b). We can find out more about this by looking at this page on the Drinkaware website: www.drinkaware.co.uk/understand-your-drinking/is-your-drinking-a-problem/binge-drinking.

- Having looked at these government guidelines, what we need to do now is talk together about what that means in terms of how many units are present in the drinks that you might have. The units and calories calculator on the Drinkaware website might help us to answer this question, available on this page: www.drinkaware.co.uk/tips-and-tools/drink-diary.

- An example on the NHS Choices website (2015) says that there are two units of alcohol in a pint of lower-strength lager (3.6% alcohol by volume; ABV), so if you were having four pints of lager, this would be eight units, which is double the government guidelines we just spoke about.

- What do you make of that information?

Doesn't everyone drink more than the guidelines?

- Sometimes you can find that, when you think about the people around you, everyone seems to use alcohol, or it feels as if there are very few people that do not drink. It can be important to think if this has always been the case. If not, what do you think has changed?

- In England, about a quarter of men said that they drank over 21 units "in an average week," and less than a quarter of women described drinking over 14 units "in an average week" (The Health and Social Care Information Centre, 2011).

- The average number of units they were having in a week was about 16 units for men and eight units for women (The Health and Social Care Information Centre, 2011).

- In a big study in the United States, it was found that about a third of people who experienced schizophrenia had problems with alcohol during their life (Regier et al., 1990).

- What do you think about this information?

What is binge drinking?

- Among different countries, the definition of binge drinking varies a little. However, the overall message is generally similar. In the United Kingdom, men are said to be "binge drinking" if they drink *eight or more* units of alcohol in a single drinking session. For women, drinking *six or more* units in a single drinking session is said to be "binge drinking" (NHS, 2014a). We can find out more about this by looking at this web page: www.drinkaware.co.uk/understand-your-drinking/is-your-drinking-a-problem/binge-drinking.

Isn't binge drinking safer, as you drink less often?

- Binge drinking usually involves drinking a quantity of alcohol in a short space of time or drinking with the end result of becoming drunk (NHS choices, 2014a).

- Binge drinking is said to be associated with risks for your mental and physical health. These can include being involved in accidents and overdose that can result in death. Binge drinking may also affect your mood and memory and sometimes leads to violent or aggressive behavior (Drinkaware, 2015b).

- We can talk more about the risks to your physical and mental health related to binge drinking if that would be useful.

Does this mean I am an alcoholic?
- The aim of our meetings is not to say whether you are an alcoholic or not; what we are looking to do is to find out what is going on for you personally and whether there is anything we could do to support you to achieve your goals. If you would like information about dependent drinking and the risks associated with this, we could look at this together.
- In terms of other people, a survey found that just under a quarter of adults in the United Kingdom were considered to be "hazardous drinkers"; of these, 16% were females and 33% males. Included within these numbers were females (2%) and males (6%) they "estimated to be harmful drinkers," who were considered to be drinking at a level where it was "likely" they would cause damage to their health (The Health and Social Care Information Centre, 2011).
- For adults in the United Kingdom aged 16–74 years, 4% of females and 9% of males were considered to be showing "some signs" of dependence on alcohol (The Health and Social Care Information Centre, 2011).
- What do you make of this?

My friend said alcohol had lots of calories in it. Is this right?
- Some people can find it useful to know the calories that are present in the alcohol that they drink. Would you like more information about this?
- There are tables we could look at that give you an idea of the amount of calories in the typical drinks people report using. For example, did you know that Drinkaware (2015c) suggest that a pint of cider (2.6 units) has 210 calories, which is the same as a sugar doughnut?
- We can find out more about this by looking at some web pages:
  - www.nhs.uk/Livewell/alcohol/Pages/calories-in-alcohol.aspx
  - www.drinkaware.co.uk/unitcalculator

How does alcohol affect my body?

- This is an interesting question; Drinkaware (2015d) outlines a number of ways in which alcohol can affect both our mental and physical health.

- Would you like to look at this further? We can find out more about this by looking at a useful web page: www.drinkaware.co.uk/check-the-facts/health-effects-of-alcohol.

Drugs and Mental Health

I've been using cannabis since I was 13, I got mental health problems in my 20's, so what could they have to do with each other?

- People often report starting to use cannabis in their teens. You have talked about using it from 13 years of age. When some 15–24-year-old Europeans were asked, they said that the most common drug they used during the previous 12 months was cannabis (EMCDDA, 2014).

- Research suggests that when you compare people not using cannabis to those who use cannabis, the age at which people using cannabis experienced psychosis was nearly 3 years younger (e.g., Large, Sharma, Compton, Slade & Nielssen, 2011).

- Some researchers say that the age you start using cannabis is important in relation to your mental health.

- One study suggests that people who started using cannabis when they were of "age 15 or younger" began to experience psychosis at a younger age than people who began using cannabis after they were 15 years of age (e.g., Di Forti et al., 2014).

- This study also found that the type of cannabis being used was important, with people using "high-potency cannabis (skunk-type)" on a daily basis beginning to first experience psychosis 6 years before people who were not using cannabis (e.g., Di Forti et al., 2014).

- What do you think about this?

Why do I get problems with mental health from cannabis when all my mates use way more and they are ok?

- It is important to say here that everyone is different; we all have different families and have different family histories of mental health. The places we grew up in and the things that we have done in our lives are all different. It is possible that, in answering this question, both our family history of mental health and the environment we grew up in could be important.

- We could look at this together using a model that can be helpful to understand how our *genes* and *life experiences* could be important. Would you like this? It is called the stress-vulnerability model (see Figure 2.1).

Additional information that may help explain the stress vulnerability model was first provided by Zubin and Spring in the 1970s (for more information, see Zubin & Spring, 1977). This model basically suggests that we all have vulnerabilities. Zubin and Spring said that there are roughly two main types of vulnerability: one that is *inborn* (e.g., genetic) and one that may be *acquired* (e.g., traumatic experiences). What they suggested was that, when the "stressors" (e.g., life events) we experience exceeds our "threshold of vulnerability," we may experience an episode of mental health difficulties.

Hence, if we think about cannabis using this stress-vulnerability model: Cannabis has been related psychosis (e.g., Van Os, Kenis & Rutten, 2010). Those who start using cannabis early (e.g., by the age of 15 years) have been found to

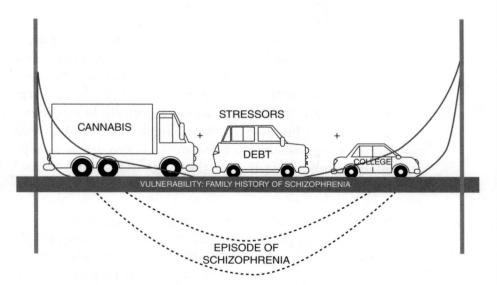

Figure 2.1 Example of using stress-vulnerability model.

experience more psychotic symptoms (Arseneault et al., 2002; Konings, Henquet, Maharajh, Hutchinson, & Van Os, 2008), and are twice as likely to develop a psychotic disorder (McGrath et al., 2010) as compared to those who start using later on. Using cannabis appears to cause those who are "vulnerable" to psychosis to experience psychosis at an earlier age (Dragt et al., 2012). *Cannabis and other environmental factors* (e.g., childhood trauma, living in an urban environment) are thought to combine with a *person's pre-existing vulnerability* (i.e., genetic) to psychosis to trigger off psychosis or schizophrenia. Recently, it has been identified that those who are more genetically vulnerable are more sensitive to the effects of cannabis (GROUP researchers, 2011). Of course, we are all individuals, and therefore all have different vulnerabilities and experience different stressors in our lives, so it can be useful to think with the client about the *genetic* and *environmental* vulnerabilities that are specifically relevant to him or her. There are a number of methods that have been used to explain this stress vulnerability model that you can use with the client—for example, using the original diagram outlining the model (in Zubin & Spring, 1977) or other metaphors such as the bucket metaphor (Brabban & Turkington, 2002). The metaphor we have used in BIMI is of a bridge (see Figure 2.1 on Page 47), as outlined by Macneil, Hasty, Conus, Berk, and Scott (2009).

Figure 2.1 illustrates that when the *stressors*, represented by the cars and the lorry, on the "bridge" (representing the client's *vulnerability*) are too heavy for the bridge or the person to withstand, they can then experience mental health difficulties (Macneil et al., 2009). In this illustrative example, the lorry representing cannabis that has just come onto the bridge is suggested as too heavy, given the strength of the bridge. This provides a good starting point to then consider in therapy about what would strengthen the bridge and how the "traffic" (i.e., stressors) could be reduced (Macneil et al., 2009).

■ As we just discussed, the research also suggests that, when compared to people who had never used cannabis, people with "a history of cannabis use" had contact with mental health services "at a younger age" when they first experienced psychosis (e.g., Di Forti et al., 2014).

- As we also discovered, the research suggests that the age at which you start using cannabis is important in relation to your mental health. What they suggest is that, when compared to people who started using cannabis later ("by age 18"), those who started using "by age 15" had more risk of experiencing symptoms of schizophrenia (e.g., Arseneault et al., 2002).
- Would you like to know more about this?

Why does everyone have so much to say about me using skunk? It is just another type of weed!
- The "Talk to Frank" website says that "skunk" is a term used to describe "a group of different types of strong herbal cannabis."
- In a Talk to Frank leaflet titled "Cannabis: Find out the facts," skunk is said to be on average over twice as strong as "traditional grass," and to have greater amounts of the key "active ingredient" found in a cannabis plant, called tetrahydrocannabinol (THC; Crown Copyright, 2009b).
- Another leaflet about cannabis, called "Cannabis: too much too often?" (2009a), says that regular use of cannabis and using it "for a long time" increases the risks to, for example, your mental and physical health, and that these risks can be "worse if you are young, you smoke a lot and you smoke strong cannabis, like skunk" (Crown Copyright, 2009a).
- What do you make of that information? Would you like more information about this? We can have a look at these leaflets and websites that might be helpful:
  - Cannabis: Find out the facts (Crown Copyright, 2009b), available at www.talktofrank.com/sites/default/files/Cannabis%20Find%20Out%20The%20Facts.pdf
  - Cannabis: Too much too often? (Crown Copyright, 2009a), available at www.talktofrank.com/sites/default/files/CannabisTMTO.pdf

What has my using drugs got to do with my being in hospital or not feeling very well mentally?
- This is a question that is quite hard to answer; perhaps we can look at what was going on for you in the run-up to your being admitted to hospital or not feeling very well mentally.

- For some people, when they look at what happened in the run-up to the hospital admission, they find that substance use may have played a part.

- It is suggested that over half of the people who experience severe mental health problems use substances (e.g., alcohol and/or drugs; Hunt, Siegfried, Morley, Sitharthan & Cleary, 2013).

- It has also been found that, when you experience severe mental health difficulties and use substances, you can have more difficulties with things such as relapses and homelessness and physical health difficulties (NICE, 2011; Hunt et al., 2013). You can also find you are admitted to psychiatric hospitals more often (NICE, 2011).

- What do you make of this information? Would you like us to find out some more information about this?

Everyone I know uses drugs. Don't most people?

- Sometimes you can find that, when you think about the people around you, it feels like everyone uses drugs, or that there are very few people who do not.

- In terms of England and Wales (2012–2013), a survey found that under 10% of adults had, in the previous 12 months, used "an illicit drug," and less than 3% of 16–59-year-olds had used a class A drug during the same time period (Home Office, 2013).

- What do you make of this information?

- In terms of what drugs were being used, when the same survey asked 16–59-year-olds about the past 12 months, cannabis was found to be the drug used most frequently, with 6.4% of the people asked having used this. The next most frequently used drugs were cocaine powder (about 2%) and then ecstasy (about 1%) (Home Office, 2013).

- Would you like to know more about this?

- When you look at how often people were using drugs, it is reported that, in 2011–2012, just over 3% of people were seen to be using drugs frequently. "Frequent drug use" was said to be typically using "more than once a month" during the previous year (NHS Statistics on drug misuse England, 2012).

- In the United States, a big research study in 1990 found that, over their lifetime, about a quarter of people who experienced schizophrenia had problems with drug use (not including alcohol) (source: Regier et al., 1990).
- What do you think about this information?

If I do not want to stop, what can I do to reduce the risks/harm?
- This is a really good question; it is important to know that if you do not want to stop using at the moment, we can still work together to look at ways to reduce the risk or harm your use may cause you. There are lots of techniques and tips that can be useful for reducing the risk and harm related to using alcohol and drugs. We can look at some of the techniques together.
- What do you think about this information?
- So, in our meetings so far, we have thought about the information you gave in the questionnaires and what that means for you and you mental health. We have compared this to what the government's lower risk guidelines are for alcohol and/or what surveys and reports suggest other people in the country are doing for both alcohol and drugs. What we can go on to look at now is where you would like to be.
- We can think together about your use of _____ [insert substance] and what you think about this and whether you would like to make any changes, such as looking at ways of reducing the harm that _____ [insert name of substance] could be causing you.
- How does that sound to you?

Do you see people who get better?
- The answer to that is YES. Services and staff working in this area meet with many people who have achieved or go on to achieve their goals. It does depend on what you mean by getting better—for some people, this means stopping using the substance and getting support from treatment, organizations, and people they know to continue not using. This is a massive achievement, and is the best way to prevent further problems related to drugs or alcohol from happening. For

some people, getting better is reducing the risk associated with their use, and once they have achieved this, some then go on to stop using, as they can see the benefits of doing this.

- ▪ Us meeting together could be an important step toward what you consider to be getting better—what do you think?

Additional Resources

Websites that might be useful
www.talktofrank.com
www.drinkaware.co.uk
www.youthspace.me

It is important to signpost clients to local and national sources of support that are relevant to them and the substances they are using.

CHAPTER THREE

Making Decisions About Change

▶ How to Decide on the Next STEP

How to Decide What STEP Is Appropriate for the Client

The content and aims of your third session will depend on the client's motivation to change. Once you have completed STEP 1 (Sessions One and Two) and provided the client with the assessment feedback, you will be aware of how the client perceives his or her substance use and whether it is seen as problematic. An additional indicator would be the client's ratings on the "importance–confidence" ruler that he or she completed during the BIMI Brief Assessment. These will help you to decide what step of the BIMI Brief Assessment is appropriate for the client next. Figure 3.1 has been developed to help facilitate this decision-making process.

If the client provided low ratings for the "importance" of changing the use of the main substance, this probably indicates that *the client does not see substance use as problematic or affecting mental health*. If this is the case, STEP 2 is probably appropriate to complete with the client next. However, it may be the case that the client provided higher ratings for the

Brief Integrated Motivational Intervention: A Treatment Manual for Co-occurring Mental Health and Substance Use Problems, First Edition. Hermine L. Graham, Alex Copello, Max Birchwood, and Emma Griffith.
© 2016 John Wiley & Sons, Ltd. Published 2016 by John Wiley & Sons, Ltd.
Companion Website: www.wiley.com/go/graham/bimi

STEP 1: Building engagment and assessment; brief assessment and feedback personalised results to the client; and provide psychoeducational information

The client *does not see* substance use as problematic or affecting mental health.
Go to STEP 2.

The client recognizes that substance use is problematic or affecting mental health *but does not want to change.*
Go to STEP 2.

The client recognizes that substance use is problematic or affecting mental health *but does not think he can change.*
Go to STEP 3.

The client recognizes that substance use is problematic or affecting mental health and *wants to change* (with or without help).
Go to STEP 3.

STEP 2: Making decisions with your client

- Identify benefits and costs of using for the present and future and identiify which of these are most important
- Identify positive/mis-held thoughts and beliefs about substance use that maintain/promote use
- Identify positive/mis-held beliefs about mental health and how it interacts with substance use
- Begin to discuss how mental health problems and substance use may interact and worsen each other
- Draw out a maintaining cycle of the triggers for drug/alcohol use, impact of substance use on mental health, relapse, and functioning
- Identify self-motivational statements of concern and intent to change

STEP 3: Change plans and social support

- Build confidence to see that change is possible, and discuss the reality of making changes
- Identify a small, realistic substance-related goal and/or personal goal that cutting down or quitting would help the client to acheive
- Look at importance and confidence in changing substance use and achieving goals
- Develop an action plan
- Identify potential setbacks and develop skills to cope with cravings, urges, and triggers for use
- Identify social support for change that can encourage attempts to change substance misuse
- Draw social network diagram

Figure 3.1 How to decide which step is best suited.

"importance" of changing the use of the main substance—that is, *the client recognizes that substance use is problematic or affecting mental health but does not want to change.* If this is the case, then STEP 2 is still probably appropriate to complete with the client next. On the other hand, *if the client recognizes that substance use is problematic or affecting mental health but does not think he or she can change,* then STEP 3 is probably appropriate to complete with the client next, to help build confidence to see that change is possible. Also, if *the client recognizes that substance use is problematic or affecting mental health and wants to change (with or without help),* then STEP 3 is still probably appropriate to complete with the client next.

Remember to keep the sessions brief, 15–30 minutes at most. The materials in STEP 2 or STEP 3 do not need to be completed in one session, but over a few sessions. It may also be the case, depending on a number of factors—such as the setting, the client's mental state, levels of motivation and engagement, and how ready the client is to change—that it is sufficient for you to only cover some of the information in STEP 2. You will need to be guided by these factors when deciding the session content and session goals. At the end of each session, remember to summarize and reflect back what has been covered, and to arrange a time for the next session.

Remember to:
- Keep the sessions brief, 15–30 minutes at most
- Decide before each session in STEP 2 and STEP 3 what the session content and session goal will be
- Only cover the material that is appropriate to the client's needs in each session
- At the end of each session, summarize what has been covered and reflect it back to the client
- Arrange a time for the next session

▶ STEP 2: Making Decisions with Your Client

Session Content	Session Goals
STEP 2: Making decisions with your client ■ Identify benefits and costs of using for the present and future, and find out which of these are most important to the client ■ Identify positive/mis-held thoughts and beliefs about substance use that promote or maintain use ■ Identify positive/mis-held thoughts and beliefs about mental health and how they interact with substance use ■ Begin to discuss how mental health problems and substance use may interact and worsen each other ■ Draw out a maintaining cycle of the triggers for drug/alcohol use, and the impact of substance use on mental health and functioning ■ Identify self-motivational statements of concern and intent to change	■ Engagement and building rapport ■ Being able to talk openly about costs and benefits of using ■ Building recognition of how positive/mis-held beliefs may promote use ■ Recognizing the maintenance cycle for mental health problems and substance use ■ Being able to state concerns about continued use and to talk about their intent to change

In STEP 2, your aim is to help the client begin to consider the *benefits* that he or she feels are gained by *continuing to use* alcohol or drugs. You will later move on to reflect on the difficulties or *costs* associated with his or her use. This will then give the client an opportunity to weigh up the benefits and costs of *using*, and consider the impact that alcohol or drug use has on mental health or admissions to hospital. Remember at the initial stage of STEP 2 that you are not discussing with the client about changing substance use; you are focusing on how things would be for him or her if he or she *continued using*, as described in the session outline.

Remember at the end of each section and session to summarize what the client has said and reflect it back to him or her, as a method of building the client's awareness.

In STEP 2, your aims are to:

■ Seek to help the client begin to consider the "benefits" that he or she feels is gained by *continuing to use* alcohol or drugs

■ You will later move on to reflect on the difficulties or "costs" associated with his or her *continued use*

▶ **Outline of Sessions**

> Remember, for these sessions you will need:
>
> ■ Worksheet 1 or Worksheet 2—"What I Enjoy About Using?"
>
> ■ Worksheet 3—"How Does My Use Sometimes Affect Me?"

You can begin this session by referring back to the information covered in Session 2:

■ When we met a couple of days ago, we looked at your results from the assessment. You said you found some of this information interesting and wanted to talk a bit more about it. What do you think about us having a look at the information together today?

■ So, shall we start with the bit that you are most interested in/concerned about?

■ Now that we have looked at this information, what do you think?

You now help the client think about what he or she enjoys about using or what keeps him or her using.

Identifying the "Benefits" of Using

What do you enjoy about using _____? Or, what keeps you using _____?

■ When people use alcohol or drugs, they often experience some benefits, and they are very aware of the things they like about using the substance or what keeps them using. So, let us start by talking about all the things you enjoy about using _____ [insert name of the substance—e.g., cannabis].

■ What are the things you like about _____ [insert name of the substance—e.g., cannabis]?

■ How do you feel that using _____ [insert name of the substance—e.g., cannabis] helps you? Is there anything more you would like to add to that?

Further prompt questions if the client says he or she no longer enjoys or likes using

■ If you do not like using, what things do you think seem to keep you using _____ [insert name of the substance— e.g., cannabis]?

■ We can start writing them down, so that we do not forget.

Use Worksheet 1 or 2 for you or the client to write them down, see pages 97 and 99). See the illustrative example given in the following:

■ What I enjoy about using *cannabis* or what keeps me using *cannabis* are:

  1 <u>I can relax with my mates</u>

  2 <u>It is amazing and sorts out my worries</u>

  3 <u>I do not get voices</u>

  4 <u>It cheers me up</u>

  5 <u>It is a habit and I have always done it</u>

■ When you look over your list, how you do feel?

  <u>It is just a habit and I have always done it</u>

■ Looking at it, does it make you think differently?

  <u>I seem to rely on it quite a bit</u>

Remember at this point to:

■ Summarize what has been said and reflect it back

Identifying Positive Thoughts and Mis-held Beliefs About Alcohol and Drugs

Now that the client is talking openly about the benefits of using, you can begin to help him or her to recognize *how positive or mis-held beliefs about the substance used may encourage continued use*. For example, "the only way I can relax is by smoking weed," and so, as you probably guessed, whenever the client feels tense or wants to relax he or she will feel an urge to use. Within cognitive behavioral therapy, these sorts of beliefs and thoughts are said to have *distortions* and *errors* within them, and are often referred to as "thinking errors" or "cognitive distortions" (Beck, Wright, Newman & Liese, 1993; Graham et al., 2004). As you may have noticed from the example "the only way I can relax is by smoking weed," this is an "absolute" statement, and there are probably other things that the client can think of that has helped him or her to relax in the past; also, they may have found that, on some occasions, after smoking cannabis, they feel a little anxious or even paranoid. However, believing or telling yourself that "the only way I can relax is by smoking weed" would entice the client to continue using.

You have already started the process of identifying these very important beliefs by asking the client about the "benefits" of using substances and recording them on Worksheet 1 or 2. These discussions can also be quite an important part of the engagement process, and will help you to understand the reasons or beliefs about the substance that keep him or her using. These will often be the thoughts or particular beliefs that block him or her from considering changing. You can continue the session by encouraging the client to review the benefits and to identify the most important benefit:

- Let us look at all the things you have listed down on your worksheet as "benefits" of using. What do you think is the most important benefit or biggest plus of using _____ [insert name of the substance—e.g., cannabis]?
- Let us go back to your list and put a star by this one.

Further prompt questions if the client is unable to identify the most important benefit
- What thoughts go through your mind just before you use _____ [insert name of the substance—e.g., cannabis]? *or*
- What do you think about using _____ [insert name of the substance—e.g., cannabis]?
- How do you think _____ [insert name of the substance— e.g., cannabis] helps you?

Let us write this down, so that we do not forget [use Worksheet 1 or 2 to write this down]:
<u>I can relax with my mates</u>.

▶ Taking Another Look at What You Think About Alcohol and Drugs

When people think about the benefits of using alcohol or drugs, they mainly think in absolute terms, for example, "whenever I drink alcohol, I always have a laugh with my mates." However, when we take a closer look at this statement, we can see that it is quite an absolute statement, which suggests that this is always true. However, as we know, because of the effects of alcohol, initially some people might feel quite jovial and disinhibited after a few drinks, but after a few more they may end up feeling quite edgy or agitated, and some people may even end up in fights. If they continue drinking, then the reality is that, at the end of the evening, they may feel quite sad, tearful, or even physically unwell. So, it is very important to encourage the client to take a second look or re-evaluate what he or she believes about the use of alcohol or drugs.

To help clients to take a second look or re-evaluate what they believe about using the substance, you will need to help them reflect on whether they "always" experience that benefit. That is, although the drug or alcohol use may meet *immediate short-term* needs, it may not always satisfy these needs in the *longer term*. Also, there may be times when the substance may have that benefit (e.g., feeling relaxed after smoking cannabis), but other times when it does not (e.g., feeling paranoid after smoking cannabis) because of other things going on in his or her life at that time. You can help the client to re-evaluate this main "benefit" by asking him or her to take a second look.

■ Let us take another look at what you said goes through your mind just before you use _____ [insert name of the substance—e.g., cannabis] and how you think _____ [insert name of the substance—e.g., cannabis] helps you.

You said when I use *cannabis, I can relax with my mates*.

- Do you think you have *always* experienced that benefit from using _____ [insert name of the substance—e.g., cannabis]?
- How do feel just after you use it? For example, how do feel later on in the day/night?
- Have there been times when you experienced different effects that are not so pleasant when using _____ [insert name of the substance—e.g., cannabis]?
- When you use _____ [insert name of the substance—e.g., cannabis], how do you find it changes your mood or mental health?
- What other effects have you experienced when using _____ [insert name of the substance—e.g., cannabis]?
- What happens after you use? How do you feel?_____ _____

> Remember at this point to:
> - Summarize what has been said and reflect it back

- So, when we took another look at the things you tend to think about cannabis, you noticed that using cannabis sometimes has different effects than you expect, such as: Sometimes I can relax with my mates when I smoke cannabis, but sometimes when I smoke with them I feel worried that they are laughing at me.
- Looking at it now, does it make you think differently?
  I guess it does not always help me relax
- Let us write this down, so that we do not forget [use Worksheet 1 or 2].

  I guess it does not always help me relax

▶ Relationship Between Mental Health Problems and Substance Use

After taking a second look at what the client thinks about alcohol or drugs, he or she may be open to reviewing the immediate and longer-term effects of his or her use. If the client is able to talk freely with you about the effects of using, then you could try to help him or her link up what his or her "triggers" (A) are for using; with what he or she "thinks" (B) about using; and what he or she "uses" and then what are the "effects" (C) of using, especially on mental health. This strategy will start to build a picture for the client about how drug or alcohol use and mental health may be connected together and impact on him or her not just immediately but later on. For example:

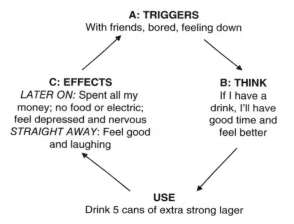

A: TRIGGERS
With friends, bored, feeling down

C: EFFECTS
LATER ON: Spent all my money; no food or electric; feel depressed and nervous
STRAIGHT AWAY: Feel good and laughing

B: THINK
If I have a drink, I'll have good time and feel better

USE
Drink 5 cans of extra strong lager

Later on in the session, this may also be an opportunity to begin to talk with the client about the research evidence that suggests there is a link between poor mental health and substance misuse (see FAQs on page 42). Alternatively, he or she may prefer to read some psycho-educational material or to look on some of the websites.

To start building awareness about the relationship between substance use and mental health, you can start by asking the client to think about the most recent time he or she used. You will need to ask if this reflects a typical time when he or she uses:

> ■ Remember: As you go through this, actually draw out the connections with the client, so they can see the picture building

Identify triggers

■ What was going on just before you used? Is that what is usually going on before you use _____ [insert name of the substance—e.g., cannabis]? _____ [write the trigger down on Worksheet 3]. These can be called your "triggers" for using.

It is important to remember that the things that trigger your client to use can be really varied and personal—that is, it could be internal, for example, such as the way they are feeling, or external, for example, related to the places they go to or certain people they spend time with (Beck et al., 1993; Graham et al., 2004).

Identify thoughts and beliefs about use

■ We discovered previously that, before you use, you usually "think" _____ [insert main positive beliefs or benefit] about using _____ [insert name of the substance—e.g., cannabis]. Let us write this down, so that we do not forget [use Worksheet 3]: _____.

How much is used?

You would have obtained this information during Session One, and it will be on the "Your Results" assessment feedback.

■ You said that you typically "use" _____ [insert quantity and the name of the substance—e.g., £5.00 worth of cannabis] and then _____ [write down on Worksheet 3].

Identify effects of use—immediate and delayed effects

■ You said that, straightaway after you use, _____ [insert what happens].

■ So, how do you feel a bit later on _____ [insert what happens], and how do you feel after that _____ [write down on Worksheet 3]?

Identify the effects of substance use on mental health/mood

■ What are the "effects" of using on your mood (and mental health) straightaway _____ [insert effects] and then later on _____ [insert effects]?

Recognizing the maintenance cycle for mental health problems and substance use

You can now summarize and take the client through the maintenance cycle or vicious cycle that you have generated together.

■ So, what you have said is that, usually just before you use _____ [insert name of substance], you are usually _____ [insert triggers] and you tend to think that _____ [insert main benefit] and that, straightaway after you use, you feel _____ [insert immediate effect] but that later on you feel _____ [insert delayed or longer-term effect] and your mood (or mental health) is _____ [insert effect].

■ Now that you have seen how your use of _____ [insert name of the substance—e.g., cannabis] affects how you feel, what do you think?

■ Had you noticed how they were connected before?

■ Looking at it now, does it make you think differently about your use of _____ [insert name of substance]?

Remember at this point to:

■ Summarize what has been said and reflect it back

■ So, when you think about some of the times when you use _____ [insert name of the substance—e.g., cannabis], you notice that there are certain effects or consequences.

■ Let us try to see if we can find any information about why that may be. I can also leave you information that you can take a look at that may explain why you feel this way after using _____ [insert name of the substance—e.g., cannabis].

At this stage, you can review with the client, if appropriate, using the FAQs or psychoeducational material, the effects of substances on mood and mental health.

▶ Reviewing Any "Costs" of Using

- We have looked at the effects of when you use _____ [insert name of the substance—e.g., cannabis]. At the beginning, when you thought about what you enjoy when you are using, and what keeps you using _____ [insert name of the substance—e.g., cannabis], you came up with a list of things that feel quite important to you.

- The things you like about using _____ [insert name of the substance—e.g., cannabis] have been important to you. They are a big factor in keeping a person using alcohol or drugs, even though the effects of using are not always positive.

- So, thinking about making any changes in how you use _____ [insert name of the substance—e.g., cannabis] might feel quite difficult as it is hard to give up something you enjoy. However, as we discovered, often the things a person enjoys may also have some "down" sides. It may be hard to spot these at first, so let us look at the case example of Sonny next and see if we can spot any difficulties that his cannabis use may be causing him.

Sonny has been smoking cannabis with his friends since he was 14 years of age. He is 28 now and smokes weed (skunk) pretty much all the time when he has money. Whenever he smokes, he feels like he cannot be bothered to do anything. He dropped out of college last year, because it felt like a waste of time, and he could not be bothered to get out of bed after smoking all evening the night before. Also, after smoking, he can start to feel quite edgy and think that kids in the street are talking about him and laughing at him, so he thinks he is better off staying in. He wants to get on with his life and find a job, but he says he cannot be bothered to look. Sonny says he never has any money to do anything as, whenever he gets any, he spends it all on weed. He has borrowed quite a bit of money from his mum and sister, and he ends up in arguments with them as he finds it hard to pay them back. He enjoys smoking as he thinks it helps him to relax and chill out, and all of his mates smoke, but he says that sometimes he can feel edgy and paranoid after smoking. Recently, he has been finding it hard to relax or sleep without smoking weed, and it gets quite tense at home. His care-coordinator and family say he used to be outgoing and really into playing sports. They feel he has changed since he started smoking weed every day. He often ends up arguing with his Mum and sister as he owes them money. Sonny has noticed that he recently has quite a chesty cough, and if he tries to run for the bus he gets out of breath really quickly.

- What difficulties do you think his cannabis use may be causing him?
  Arguments with his family
  Spending all his money on weed
  Dropping out of college and not looking for the job he wants

- Some of the difficulties may seem less obvious such as:
  Feeling like he cannot be bothered to do anything
  Borrowing money from his family
  Chesty cough
  Getting out of breath quickly
  Finding it hard to relax or go to sleep without cannabis
  Getting edgy and paranoid and not wanting to go out

Difficulties my use may be causing?
- So, let us think a bit more about any difficulties or problems you think your _____ [insert name of the substance— e.g., cannabis] use may be causing.

- Let us write them down, so we do not forget [use Worksheet 1 or 2 and add to the second section]: _____
  _____.

Further prompt questions, if the client cannot think of any difficulties
- If you cannot think of any difficulties, first of all let us think about what concerns others (e.g., mum, dad, brothers, sisters, other relatives, girlfriend, boyfriend, friends,

care co-ordinator, mental health team, psychiatrist) may have about your use of _____ [insert name of the substance—e.g., cannabis].

- Have there been times in the past when you or anyone else may have been concerned about the impact that your use was having on you?

- If you do not think anyone is worried about your use, or if you do not mind if they are, how does using _____ [insert name of the substance—e.g., cannabis] affect how much money you have? Your physical health? Your mood? Your mental health?

- Sometimes a person may not be able to see any immediate problems with their _____ [insert name of the substance—e.g., cannabis] use, so it is useful to think further into the future.

- So, think about if you keep using _____ [insert name of the substance—e.g., cannabis], as you were before you came into hospital or started to feel unwell, what problems might this cause for you 6 months or a year down the road?

- Let us write them down, so we do not forget [use Worksheet 1 or 2].

- Difficulties that my use of _____ [insert name of the substance—e.g., cannabis] may be causing:

  1 _____

  2 _____

  3 _____

  4 _____

  5 _____

- When you look over your list, how do you feel?

  _____

- Looking at it, does it make you think differently?

  _____

■ So, if you had to sum up your main concern, or the ones that those who are concerned about you may have, what would it be? Let us write this down, so that we do not forget [use Worksheet 1 or 2]:

I/They feel concerned that my _____ [insert name of the substance—e.g., cannabis] use may _____.

Let us think now about what you think might need to change to reduce the level of concern. What would you need to do? Would you need to cut down? Stop all together? Change the way you use? Let us write this down, so that we do not forget [use Worksheet 1 or 2]. To reduce the level of concern, I would need to _____.

Remember at this point to:

■ Summarize what has been said and reflect it back
■ Spend time trying out and identifying strategies for coping with cravings and urges that work for the client

---

CHAPTER FOUR

Change

▶ STEP 3: Change Plans and Social Support

Session Content	Intervention Goals
STEP 3: Change Plans and Social Support	
Developing a change plan:	
▪ Identify a realistic substance-related goal and/or personal goal that cutting down or quitting would help the client achieve	▪ Helping change to feel possible
▪ Look at importance and confidence in changing substance use and achieving the goal	
▪ Develop an action plan	▪ Identifying potential setbacks (e.g., cravings/urges and social network)
▪ Identify skills to cope with cravings, urges, and triggers for use	▪ Being able to use skills to cope with setbacks, including cravings, urges, and triggers for use
Social support for change:	
▪ Identify social supports that can encourage attempts to change substance misuse	
▪ Draw social network diagram	▪ Provide social support for change

In STEP 3, your aim is to help *build the client's confidence to make the change that he or she wants and to see that change is possible.* It will be important to work through with the client the

Brief Integrated Motivational Intervention: A Treatment Manual for Co-occurring Mental Health and Substance Use Problems, First Edition. Hermine L. Graham, Alex Copello, Max Birchwood, and Emma Griffith.

reality of what changing in alcohol and drug use would be like and develop strategies that will make change feel more possible.

You can start the process by first reviewing why the client would like to make a change and what change he or she would like (if the client completed STEP 2, see "Reviewing any costs of using," page 65).

As outlined previously, the client probably has particular things that he or she wants out of life right now. One of them is probably "not being admitted into a psychiatric hospital again," or to feel mentally well again. It is possible that drug or alcohol misuse has played a part in his or her current hospital admission, or in his or her feeling mentally unwell. Therefore, future alcohol or drug use may well stand in the way of the client achieving the goal of "not being admitted again" or of feeling mentally well again. Other things that he or she may want in life can be personal or life goals, which we all want (e.g., getting a job, learning to drive, going on a holiday, starting a relationship, living independently, making friends, going out socially, having more money to buy food or pay bills, not being in debt to dealers, and appropriate reduction of medication). It is possible that his or her use of alcohol or drugs has prevented the achievement of these goals. So, to continue the process of developing a change plan with the client, you will also need to jointly identify a small, realistic, substance-related goal and/or personal goal that cutting down or quitting would help the client achieve.

In STEP 3, your aims are to:

■ Help change to feel possible

■ Identify a small, realistic, substance-related goal and/or personal goal that cutting down or quitting would help the client achieve

■ Identify social supports that can encourage the client's attempts to change

---

> Remember, for these sessions you will need:
> ■ Worksheet 4—"Taking Steps Toward My Goal"

■ Now that you have considered what you would need to do to reduce the level of concern about your _____ [insert name of substance] use, let us think about what you think could be gained from making this change. What would these be (e.g., having more money, taking driving lessons)?

Taking Steps Toward My Goals

■ Can we call the things that you could gain from making this change as your "goal" (e.g., having more money to be able to buy food)? Which goal should we focus on first? Which one feels more achievable as a first step?

■ Let us write them down, so that we do not forget [use Worksheet 4]: _____

■ OK, so let us write down where you are now (e.g., in £60 debt to dealers).

■ Let us break down your goal into steps that feel a bit more achievable on a day-to-day basis (e.g., when I get paid, first of all, I will buy £10 worth of food, then pay £20 off my debt, and spend £20 on cannabis rather than £30).

■ What could the next step be in achieving your goal of having more money to buy food (e.g., when I get paid next time, first of all, I will buy £15 worth of food, then pay £20 off my debt, and spend £15 on cannabis rather than £20)?

■ And what would your next step be? (e.g., when I get paid next time, first of all I will buy £20 worth of food, then pay £20 off my debt, and spend £10 on cannabis rather than £15)?

■ And your next step (e.g., when I get paid next time, first of all I will buy £25 worth of food, then I will have paid off my debt, and I can spend £10 on cannabis and save £15 toward a driving lesson)?

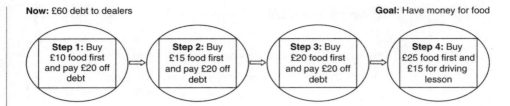

Now: £60 debt to dealers   **Goal:** Have money for food

Step 1: Buy £10 food first and pay £20 off debt

Step 2: Buy £15 food first and pay £20 off debt

Step 3: Buy £20 food first and pay £20 off debt

Step 4: Buy £25 food first and £15 for driving lesson

■ When you look over your steps to achieve your goal, how do you feel?

_____

■ Looking at it, does it make you think differently?

_____

> Remember at this point to:
> ■ Summarize what has been said and reflect it back

Coping with Setbacks

■ Let us think of any possible setbacks (e.g., cravings/urges, friends, dealers) that may stand in the way of you achieving your goal. What could these be?

Let us write them down, so we do not forget [use Worksheet 3]: <u>When I get paid, I see the dealer first, and he wants me to pay off the £60 I owe him straightaway</u>

■ OK, let us think together about how you could tackle this situation: <u>I could go with a non-drug-using friend or care-coordinator to collect my money and buy my food first, and only take £40 to the dealers</u>

■ Are there any other possible setbacks you can see with this? <u>I may feel tempted to buy £20 worth of cannabis and get £20 more on credit</u>

■ OK, let us think together about how you could tackle this situation: <u>I could go with a non-drug-using friend, or I could take a picture of the car I would love to get when I pass my driving test and remind myself of why getting into debt with dealers never works out well for me</u>

- Are there any other possible setbacks you can see? <u>I'm craving so much for more cannabis that I go back to get more on credit from the dealers</u>

- OK, let us think together about how you could tackle this situation: _____.

Strategies to Cope with Cravings and Urges

You may find it useful at this stage to introduce the client to some simple strategies to cope with carvings and urges to use. A range of strategies that the client may find helpful are described here. It is important to encourage the client to identify the one(s) that is most suited to him or her and to practice the strategy in the session to build confidence in using it.

- *Imagery*: Let us try an exercise to help you cope with urges. Imagine you are standing, waiting on a platform at a train station, and your "urge to get more cannabis" is painted all over the outside of the train like graffiti; imagine the train coming into the station, stopping at the platform, and then moving out of the train station with your "urge." As you see the train moving away with the "urge" on, notice the urge is getting smaller and smaller and fading away.

- *Distraction*: Another strategy may be to go off and do something else that really occupies your mind and time until the urge passes, such as watching TV, listening to music, playing computer games, or talking to someone you find supportive.

- *Relaxation*: Some people also find that trying to relax by breathing in the "urge" to a count of seven and then breathing it out and letting go to a count of 11 really helps.

- *What I tell myself*: Sometimes when we make a decision to change something, we may still feel a bit torn. We can see all the reasons why changing would be a good, but on the other hand we may feel reluctant to change, or that we are not going to be able to succeed. Let us go back to the case of Sonny:

Sonny feels "concerned that his cannabis use is causing arguments in his home, and that his mum will finally kick him out and he'll be on the streets." He thinks that "to reduce the level of concern I have that my mum will kick me out, I need to cut down how much weed I am smoking and get a job." When Sonny thinks about changing, he thinks:

The positives of changing are:

1 My mum will be pleased
2 My mum will not kick me out
3 I will have more money in my pocket to buy the things I want

The negatives of changing are:

1 I will not be able to chill out with my mates and smoke
2 I will not be able to get to sleep
3 I like smoking weed
4 I have tried before and failed

■ What do you think would help Sonny feel more able to succeed?
■ Sometimes what we tell ourselves may prevent us from succeeding—for example, if Sonny tells himself "there is no point in trying to change; I have tried before and failed." However, if Sonny takes another look at what he is telling himself, he may remember that he had been able to cut down his cannabis use when he had to pay off a few debts. He had also stopped smoking for 2 months when he was last in hospital. Sonny was then able to tell himself, "I have been able to make some changes in the past, but the willpower was not enough. This time, I have a better chance of success as I have some support and a plan."

Remember at this point to:
■ Summarize what has been said and reflect it back

It is important to spend time with the client planning and practicing how to deal with the identified potential setbacks, as these can often derail the client from achieving his or her goal. The result is often a loss of self-efficacy; that is, confidence that he or she can actually make a change. This may have happened to the client in the past, and he or she may believe that: "I'm not sure that I can change or achieve my goal, too many things stand in my way."

Here, you can introduce the client to a further imagery exercise.

- *Imagery* (Hayes, 2005; Follette & Pistorello, 2007): Another exercise that you might find helpful is to imagine that you are the driver of a bus, and you know where you are heading to (your goal/destination). But you have many pesky passengers on the bus who constantly bother you and prevent you from driving your bus. What could you do?

- Let us imagine who/what is on your bus that may make achieving your goal difficult (e.g., cravings, drug dealers, friends who I drink alcohol or use drugs with, boredom). How could you deal with each of these pesky passengers (e.g., share your goal with them, put their seatbelts on, ask them to leave you alone and move to the back of the bus, ask them to get off the bus if they are going to distract you, ask someone else to come and help you manage the passengers)?

> Remember at this point to:
> - Summarize what has been said and reflect it back

- So, in sum, you have been able to identify a goal that you would like to achieve, you can see possible setbacks, but you have been able to identify things that might help, so that you can move forward.

- How do you feel about what we have discussed? _____

_____

▶ Social Support for Change

Alcohol and drug use are often social activities, and for some clients they may be the main means of social contact and interaction. However, importantly, non-substance-using social networks are more likely to encourage and or support positive change in alcohol and drug use and prevent people from slipping back into problem use. So, in STEP 3, a vital part of developing a change plan involves identifying social support for change and goal attainment.

You can encourage the identification of social support for the client's attempts to change alcohol or drug use through the client's *own natural social network*, or by introducing him or her to *groups in the community that can offer positive support*. The session outline focuses on using the clients' own social network. However, in addition, you may be able to identify with his or her supportive groups or services in his or her local community. Strategies for identifying supportive social networks are introduced in these sessions. Further information on developing and building supportive social networks can be found in the treatment manual for social behavior and network therapy (Copello, Orford, Hodgson, & Tober, 2009).

▶ Developing Supportive Social Networks

Outline of Sessions

- Let us start by looking at who is important to you, and think about how they might help you achieve your goals.
- Draw a social network diagram. Start with a question such as: "Can you think of all the people that are important to you?"

It is useful to start to draw the social network diagram collaboratively with the client, such as the one in Figure 4.1. You place the client at the center and draw other members of the client's social network around him or her. Wherever possible, use people's names, as it makes the network more real and relevant to the client. For each person in the network, indicate whether or not he or she would be supportive of the client making the change or achieving the goal, who the client would be willing to tell about his or her change plan, and who in the client's view would support him or her. At this stage, try to include as many people as possible in the network diagram to start with. Think about local support groups or organizations that may also offer support. Do not engage in a detailed discussion about each individual member too soon as the initial emphasis is on having as many members of the social network included as possible. It is

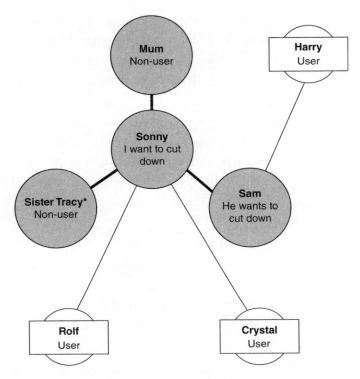

Figure 4.1 An example of a social network diagram.

important to identify everyone in the social network at this early stage, as even those with whom there is not much contact at the moment could become potential supporters in the future, and those who encourage continued substance use could be made to be less influential. Certain questions can help the exploration:

■ How often do you see him or her?

■ Let us note down all the people in your network who use drugs or alcohol.

■ Of the people around you, which ones do you think would be supportive of you making a change in your use of _____ [insert name of substance—e.g., cannabis]? Let us make a note of them.

■ Which people are more likely to encourage you to keep on using?

■ Which one of these people could you speak to about the goal that you have set and would be willing to encourage you? Let us make a note of such people by their name (e.g., I'll tell Sam and my sister Tracy).

■ Let us review each person in turn about how specifically they can help you with your goal.

Discuss with the client how he or she can start the process of talking to the person who he or she has identified as someone he or she can tell about his or her goal. Practice using role-play to practice how the client might go about initiating the conversation, and explore strategies to cope with the discussion not going as planned.

> Remember at this point to:
> ■ Summarize what has been said and reflect it back
> ■ Develop the social network diagram collaboratively, including as many members of your client's network as possible

It may be useful to provide the identified family members or supportive social network members with some information that would help engage them in the process, and get them to think about how they can best offer support to the client and access support themselves. This is detailed in the following section. This information is also available in the appendix as two handouts.

▶ Helpful Information for Family Members or Supportive Social Network Members

This section provides strategies that will encourage family members or supportive social network members to think about how the situation is affecting them and others in the family or network in terms of the stresses faced. In addition, family members or supportive social network members will be encouraged to consider the range of feelings that they are experiencing, and strategies are suggested for how to aim to deal with these in a helpful way. The following information can be given as a handout for family members or close friends.

Understanding Cannabis, Alcohol, and Other Substance Use, and How It Impacts on Family and Others

This information section is aimed at helping you understand and respond to the challenging experience of having someone close to you who experiences substance misuse and mental health problems, and to think about ways in which you can look after yourself as well as offer support to the person you are concerned about. If you are reading this, it is more than likely that a friend or loved one has developed a problem with substance use in addition to mental health problems. On the other hand, you may be unsure about whether there is a problem, whether the problem is a serious one, but yet you are worried. Finding out that your relative has got a substance problem is unlikely to happen as a single event. You may have been wondering for a while if he or she has been using drugs. Perhaps his or her behavior has at times been unpredictable or changeable in ways that are difficult to explain or fully understand. We also know that, when substance use problems also happen alongside mental health problems, this combination can be complex and challenging.

Let us focus on your experience to start with. We know from research and from what family members or supportive social network members have told us that their experiences can include, for example, being concerned about the person's health and safety, the financial implications of drug use, finding the person difficult to live with, incidents and crises at home, and a lot of worry about the impact on family or friendships. All of these are common experiences that families describe at some length when asked about living with a close relative with a substance use problem or a substance use and mental health problem combined.

One of the most important things to keep in mind as a family member or a supportive social network member in these situations is to not panic. It is likely that, in time, you can find a way of understanding what is happening that will be helpful. A good starting point is to understand your own experience, as this is mostly within your control (although at times it may not feel like this!).

Do Others Experience Similar Problems?

Before thinking and looking more closely at your own experience, it is worth considering how common these problems are. Living with someone with a drug or alcohol problem is a very common experience. It happens to a lot of people, although it is mostly hidden because people do not like to talk about this to others. A common feeling reported by family members or supportive friends is the shame and worry about what other people may think of the person who is using drugs, of you, or of the family as a whole. If you feel like this, it is problematic because it will make you hide the experience and increase your isolation. In addition, we know that disagreements can take place between different family members or friends when these problems are discussed. This again can increase your sense of hopelessness and isolation, and the feeling that you are dealing with this problem on your own, which in turn can be a really challenging experience. In fact, living with someone with a substance misuse problem and being affected by this experience is so common that it ranks among the most commonly reported forms of severe and chronic stress in the Western world. Here, we are talking about millions of people rather than thousands. In fact, in a recent study we conducted, we estimated that there are over 1 million adult family members significantly affected by serious drug problems, including cannabis, of someone in the family in the United Kingdom. The number increases exponentially if we consider alcohol problems as well. Hence, one of the most important things to remind yourself, if you are feeling like this, is that *YOU ARE NOT ALONE.*

How Do I Make Sense of This?

Having established that this is a common experience, as we were saying earlier, it is important to think about the aspects of the experience that can be under your control even though they may not feel controllable at present. Gaining some sense of control and understanding of your experience will help you feel less confused, and will allow you to identify and name some of the roller coaster of emotions that you may be feeling at present (e.g., anger, despair, and fear). Being able to name those emotions and identify why they are happening and where they come from can make you feel better, even when the drug problem of your relative has not changed much or at all. First, you can try and identify a situation or behavior related to your experience, for example, your son coming back home late at night and appearing quite confused and "stoned." Describe the event as clearly and specifically as you can (e.g., Martin comes home very late and appears to be "stoned"). You may even go onto describe some of the signs that make you think this (e.g., he is giddy, does not make sense, and his eyes look very puffy). Next, try to identify what you felt when this happened. Again, try and be very specific (e.g., "I feel really *annoyed* when this happens but also *frightened* and *upset*," as opposed to "I feel like my world is collapsing," which is a rather broad and abstract description). In the first example, you are naming the feelings and making them clear, the first step toward dealing with them. You can also explore some of those feelings in more depth. You can try and think about what you are frightened of, or about what is making you feel upset. For example, we know that a lot of family members or supportive social network members fear for the health and safety of their loved one and feel upset because they feel let down and feel that they cannot trust the person.

At times, you may start wondering whether the only positive thing that can happen is that your loved one seeks help for his or her alcohol or drug use. While this would clearly be a very positive step, it may not happen for a while. However, we know that family members or supportive friends can improve their experience and come to terms with some of the feelings of despair by working on their own understanding of the situation, even in those cases where the person does not access help straightaway or change in the short term. It may also be important at this stage for you to consider what the impact is on other members of the family or network of friends of the person using alcohol or drugs.

Why Do I Feel So Stressed?

The next area that is important to consider at this early stage is the *strain* that you, as a family member or a friend, may be experiencing. We know that family members of people with addiction problems have high symptoms of physical and psychological stress. Physical symptoms include experiences such as loss of appetite, difficulty sleeping, and high blood pressure. Psychological symptoms include feeling anxious or depressed, increasing your own intake of substances by drinking or smoking more, and a general sense of worry that is with you most of the time. However, starting to talk to people who are in a position to help may be a very important first step for you to take. Being able to make sense of your experience may allow you to help and support your loved one from a calmer and positive stance.

To Sum It Up

If you have read up to this point, we hope that this would have helped you to think more about your situation and the problems that you are facing. We hope also that you have been able to identify more specifically and clearly the aspects of the situation that are contributing to your experience of stress and worry, and also considered some of the possible symptoms of stress that you are experiencing as an affected family member or close friend. This is a very important step in order to begin to take control of your situation and your experience, and to plan ways of responding to both your needs and those of your loved one in a helpful way.

The most important thing to remind yourself is that *YOU ARE NOT ALONE*, that there are millions of other people experiencing similar situations, and that some of the most frightening thoughts and feelings you have had are the result of the stress that is arising from your understandable concern and worry about your loved one. Beginning to come to grips with what is going on for yourself and for your relative or friend is the first step in planning what to do in response.

Depending on where you live, there will be organizations that offer support and, in some parts of the world, self-help groups for family members affected by the drug and mental health problems of a relative. In the United Kingdom and other countries, for example, there will be Al-Anon groups supporting families dealing with alcohol misuse and Families Anonymous groups supporting families dealing with drug misuse. Adfam, again in the United Kingdom, is a national organization working in a range of ways to support families affected by drug use, and can offer advice about local services.

Some books that you may be interested in reading

Mueser, K. T. & Gingerich, S. (2006). *The Complete Family Guide to Schizophrenia: Helping Your Loved One Get the Most Out of Life*. New York: Guilford Press. This book is focused on schizophrenia and has an excellent section devoted to the use of alcohol and drugs in those with severe mental health problems.

Books that cover the impact of drug and alcohol use on families and different family members

Barnard, M. (2007). *Drug Addiction and Families*. London: Jessica Kingsley.

Orford, J. (2012). *Addiction Dilemmas. Family Experiences in Literature and Research and Their Lessons for Practice*. Chichester: Wiley-Blackwell.

Trimingham, T. (2009). *Not My Family, Never My Child: What To Do If Someone You Love Is a Drug User*. Australia: Allen & Unwin.

You will be able to find additional resources quoted in these books or related websites.

How Can I Best Support My Family Member or Friend?

Keeping communication open

Your family member, loved one, or friend may have approached you as someone who he or she thinks can offer support to make a change or achieve an identified important goal. This can be helpful for both yourself and the person with the substance misuse and mental health problem, as it means that you will be able to communicate more openly with each other, and you may be able to offer your support and encouragement, which we know is important in helping people change substance use habits and achieve their goals. Keeping communication open is an important aim.

Supporting his or her goal

Listen to what your loved one may tell you about his or her goal and talk together if necessary with help from your loved one's

Clinician about the possible ways in which you may support his or her goals. Your loved one's goals may involve, for example, trying to "avoid admission to a mental health unit in the future," and part of this may involve trying to not use substances. Other goals may involve personal aims—for example, getting a job, learning to drive, or getting fitter. Your loved one will be encouraged to identify a small, realistic, substance-related or personal goal, and to think about people who are important and can offer support in achieving this goal. You can support this goal at the simplest level by being genuinely encouraging or, at a more practical level, by helping him or her identify and pursue ways of achieving the goal—for example, visiting the job center together or exploring together ways of increasing physical exercise and getting fitter.

Boosting Change

▶ Booster Session Content

Session Content	Intervention Goals
■ Review self-motivational statements of concern and intent to change	■ Consolidate motivation and transfer skills from BIMI to the community
■ Review action plan	■ Review progress with substance-related goals and skills to tackle setbacks
■ Review social support for change and introduce to community-based treatment	■ Link participants with community-based substance misuse treatment

At the final session with the client, you will need to arrange a "booster session." This session is suggested to occur *1 month after the final session*. If the client was in hospital at the time BIMI was delivered, it can be while he or she is still an inpatient. This session aims to help consolidate the client's motivation by encouraging him or her to review and remember the sessions you had, including: any changes in thinking about substance use, the links discovered between substance use and mental health, and other effects and additional goals. It also seeks to transfer the skills from BIMI to the community by introducing them to community-based

Brief Integrated Motivational Intervention: A Treatment Manual for Co-occurring Mental Health and Substance Use Problems, First Edition. Hermine L. Graham, Alex Copello, Max Birchwood, and Emma Griffith.
© 2016 John Wiley & Sons, Ltd. Published 2016 by John Wiley & Sons, Ltd.
Companion Website: www.wiley.com/go/graham/bimi

substance misuse treatment and by actively linking clients into community support routinely integrated within community mental health services. This session is also an opportunity to discuss with the client how to integrate what has been learned during the sessions into his or her relapse plan and ongoing treatment plan. This could include the effects of substance use on mental health, goals for substance use, and community-based substance misuse treatment options.

In the booster session, your aims are to:

- Consolidate the client's motivation and decision to make a change

- Review progress with the client's goal and tackle any setbacks

- Link client with any additional social supports and treatment options

---

▶ Booster Session Outline

- We met quite a few times when you were admitted to hospital (or not feeling mentally well), and spent time talking about your use of _____ [insert name of substance—e.g., cannabis].

- How have things gone for you in relation to your use of _____ [insert name of substance—e.g., cannabis] since we last met?

- Let us remind ourselves of what we focused on during our session.

At this stage, you will need to review the key steps and issues covered during your previous sessions and offer support, if necessary, to help the client build on his or her initial motivation to change. If necessary, briefly revisit or go to STEP 2 to remind the client of what he or she thought the "benefits" and "costs" associated with continued use were (Worksheet 1 or 2), and the "effects my use sometimes has on me" (Worksheet 3). Re-establish with the client motivational statements of concern and intention to change. If the client is in agreement, discuss how the effects of substance use on mental health, which had been identified, can be integrated into his or her relapse plan and ongoing treatment plan.

Review Self-Motivational Statements of Concern and Intention to Change

- At that time, you felt that you wanted to [insert what client wanted to do about his or her substance use]

  _____

- Is that how you still feel? Or do you feel differently now?

  _____

- What would help you now?

  _____

> Remember at this point to:
> - Summarize what has been covered previously and how the client feels now and reflect it back

Review the Maintenance Cycle for Mental Health Problems and Substance Use

It may be helpful to summarize and take the client through the maintenance cycle or vicious cycle that you had generated together.

- So, when we discussed this earlier, you noticed that sometimes there is a connection between what you use and how you feel. What you have said was that, usually just before you use _____ [insert name of substance], you are usually _____ [insert triggers] and you tend to think that _____ [insert main benefit], and that straightaway after you use you feel _____ [insert immediate effect], but that later on you feel _____ [insert delayed or longer-term effect] and your mood (or mental health) is _____ [insert effect].

- Is that still how you feel they are connected?

> Remember at this point to:
> - Summarize what has been covered previously and how the client feels now and reflect it back

It might be necessary to briefly revisit or go to STEP 3 to remind the client of what he or she had decided was the goal to work toward. You can do this by reviewing the "Taking Steps Toward My Goal" worksheet (Worksheet 3), and focusing on developing helpful strategies to manage any setbacks that may have arisen. Discuss how these goals could be integrated into his or her ongoing treatment plan.

Review Progress with Substance-related Goal and Skills to Tackle Setbacks

- When we met earlier, you said that you wanted to [insert what client wanted to do about his or use]

  _____

- Is that still how you feel? Or do you feel differently now?

  _____

- How have you gotten on with taking steps toward your goal?

  _____

- What else would help you now?

  _____

Remember at this point to:

- Summarize what has been covered previously and how the client feels now and reflect it back

---

Review Social Support for Change

- At that time, you felt that _____ [insert name of supportive social network member] could provide you with support in achieving your goals.

- Is that how you still feel? Or do you feel differently now?

  _____

- What other support would you need to help you make the changes you would like? _____

  _____

If necessary, revisit/re-do the clients' social network diagram and re-establish with the client his or her sources of support.

> Remember at each point to:
> ■ Summarize what has been covered previously and how the client feels now and reflect it back

▶ Link in with Community-based Substance Misuse Treatment Services

Toward the end of the session, introduce the client to community-based substance misuse services and any additional support appropriate to support him or her. The reason for actively linking the client with appropriate substance misuse treatment, at this stage, is to ensure that he or she has support and can continue to build on his or her motivation to change and take steps toward the self-identified goal and maintain changes within his or her community setting.

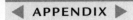

Worksheets and Handouts

BIMI—Brief Assessment Sheet

	Alcohol	Cannabis	Crack Cocaine	Cocaine Powder	Legal Highs	Heroin	Illicit Methadone	Amphetamine	Other
Have you used this in the past 30 days?									
When did you last use this?									
What is the amount you use on a typical day?									
How much do you spend on this on a typical day?									

Brief Integrated Motivational Intervention: A Treatment Manual for Co-occurring Mental Health and Substance Use Problems, First Edition. Hermine L. Graham, Alex Copello, Max Birchwood, and Emma Griffith.
© 2016 John Wiley & Sons, Ltd. Published 2016 by John Wiley & Sons, Ltd.
Companion Website: www.wiley.com/go/graham/bimi

	Alcohol	Cannabis	Crack Cocaine	Cocaine Powder	Legal Highs	Heroin	Illicit Methadone	Amphetamine	Other
What route? Oral Smoke/ chase Snort/sniff Intravenous									
During a typical week, how frequently would you use this?									
How old were you when you first used this?									
Which substance is the *main* one you use?									

Source: Drug and alcohol use in the past 30 days (based on MAP, Marsden et al., 1998)

AUDIT

Questions	Scoring System					Your Score
	0	*1*	*2*	*3*	*4*	
1 How often do you have a drink containing alcohol?	Never	Monthly or less	2–4 times per month	2–3 times per week	4+ times per week	
2 How many units of alcohol do you drink on a typical day when you are drinking?	1–2	3–4	5–6	7–8	10+	
3 How often have you had six or more units if female, or eight or more if male, on a single occasion in the last year?	Never	Less than monthly	Monthly	Weekly	Daily or almost daily	
4 How often during the last year have you found that you were not able to stop drinking once you had started?	Never	Less than monthly	Monthly	Weekly	Daily or almost daily	
5 How often during the last year have you failed to do what was normally expected from you because of your drinking?	Never	Less than monthly	Monthly	Weekly	Daily or almost daily	
6 How often during the last year have you needed an alcoholic drink in the morning to get yourself going after a heavy drinking session?	Never	Less than monthly	Monthly	Weekly	Daily or almost daily	
7 How often during the last year have you had a feeling of guilt or remorse after drinking?	Never	Less than monthly	Monthly	Weekly	Daily or almost daily	
8 How often during the last year have you been unable to remember what happened the night before because you had been drinking?	Never	Less than monthly	Monthly	Weekly	Daily or almost daily	
9 Have you or somebody else been injured as a result of your drinking?	No		Yes, but not in the last year		Yes, during the last year	
10 Has a relative or friend, doctor, or other health worker been concerned about your drinking or suggested that you cut down?	No		Yes, but not in the last year		Yes, during the last year	

Source: Saunders et al., 1993

SDS

Tell your client: "Please think of your use of _____ during a recent period of using when you answer these questions."

1. Did you think that your use of _____ was out of control?

☐ 0. Never/ almost never ☐ 1. Sometimes ☐ 2. Often ☐ 3. Always/ nearly always

2. Did the prospect of missing a fix (or dose) make you anxious or worried?

☐ 0. Never/ almost never ☐ 1. Sometimes ☐ 2. Often ☐ 3. Always/ nearly always

3. Did you worry about your use of _____?

☐ 0. Never/ almost never ☐ 1. Sometimes ☐ 2. Often ☐ 3. Always/ nearly always

4. Did you wish you could stop?

☐ 0. Never/ almost never ☐ 1. Sometimes ☐ 2. Often ☐ 3. Always/ nearly always

5. How difficult did you find it to stop or go without _____?

☐ 0. Not difficult ☐ 1. Quite difficult ☐ 2. Very difficult ☐ 3. Impossible

Source: Gossop et al., 1995.

IMPORTANCE–CONFIDENCE RULER

Ask your client: On a scale of 0–10, how important is it right now for you to change your use of _____ [insert name of substance]?

Importance: 0 _____ 10

On a scale of 0–10, if you decide to change, how confident are you that you would succeed?

Confidence: 0 _____ 10

MOOD
PHQ-9

Name _____ Date _____

Over the *last 2 weeks*, how often have you been bothered by any of the following problems?	Not at all	Several days	More than half the days	Nearly every day
1. Little interest or pleasure in doing things	0	1	2	3
2. Feeling down, depressed, or hopeless	0	1	2	3
3. Trouble falling or staying asleep, or sleeping too much	0	1	2	3
4. Feeling tired or having little energy	0	1	2	3
5. Poor appetite or overeating	0	1	2	3
6. Feeling bad about yourself—or that you are a failure or have let yourself or your family down	0	1	2	3
7. Trouble concentrating on things, such as reading the newspaper or watching television	0	1	2	3
8. Moving or speaking so slowly that other people could have noticed; or the opposite—being so fidgety or restless that you have been moving around a lot more than usual	0	1	2	3
9. Thoughts that you would be better off dead or of hurting yourself in some way	0	1	2	3

(For office coding: total score _____ = _____ + _____ + _____)

If you checked off *any* problems, how *difficult* have these problems made it for you to do your work, take care of things at home, or get along with other people?

Not difficult at all	Somewhat difficult	Very difficult	Extremely difficult
☐	☐	☐	☐

GAD-7

Over the <u>last 2 weeks</u>, how often have you been bothered by the following problems?	Not at all	Several days	More than half the days	Nearly every day
1. Feeling nervous, anxious or on edge	0	1	2	3
2. Not being able to stop or control worrying	0	1	2	3
3. Worrying too much about different things	0	1	2	3
4. Trouble relaxing	0	1	2	3
5. Being so restless that it is hard to sit still	0	1	2	3
6. Becoming easily annoyed or irritable	0	1	2	3
7. Feeling afraid as if something awful might happen	0	1	2	3

Total _____ = Add _____ + _____ + _____
Score   Columns

If you checked off <u>any</u> problems, how <u>difficult</u> have these problems made it for you to do your work, take care of things at home, or get along with other people?

Not difficult at all	Somewhat difficult	Very difficult	Extremely difficult
☐	☐	☐	☐

The PHQ-9 and GAD-7 questionnaires have been developed by Drs. Robert L. Spitzer, Janet B. W. Williams, Kurt Kroenke, and colleagues, with an educational grant from Pfizer Inc. No permission required to reproduce, translate, display, or distribute.

BIMI ASSESSMENT FEEDBACK—*YOUR RESULTS*
Diagnosis: _____ Substance of choice: _____

Part 1
ALCOHOL

Alcohol	Your current use	United Kingdom (%)	Lower risk guidelines
Per day			Females 2–3 Males: 3–4
Per week			
Amount spent (£)			
AUDIT score			

Impact of alcohol at current pattern of use:

DRUGS

Drug	Your current use (per week)	Amount spent (£) (per week)
Cannabis		
Crack/ cocaine		
Ecstasy		
Heroin		
Other		
Total spent (£)		
Dependence score		

Part 2

_____ [insert name of substance] USE: You said you were using _____ [insert quantity used and frequency of use], which cost about _____ [insert financial cost]. When we have a look at the drug/alcohol use across the country for adults, _____ [insert relevant information related to prevalence for relevant country in the general population] _____. Research suggests that about _____ [e.g., insert general population percentage] _____ use more than once a month. What do you make of that information? Is it what you expected, or different from what you expected? Your results suggested that your use of _____ [insert name of substance] is at a level that is often associated with _____ [insert information concerning level of use from AUDIT/SDS]. What do you make of this result?

MOTIVATION TO CHANGE: Your results suggest you felt that it was _____ [insert statement based on the rating on the importance scale], but also felt that you were _____ [insert statement based on the rating on the confidence scale] confident that you could make a change in your _____ [insert name of substance] use if you decided you wanted to. Is this still the case?

YOUR MOOD: Your scores suggested that, at that time, you were feeling _____ [insert statement from anxiety scores] and _____ [insert statement from depression scores] in mood.

WHAT RESEARCH SUGGESTS ABOUT THE IMPACT OF _____ [insert name of substance] ON MENTAL HEALTH
One of the leaflets from the _____ [insert name of the website—i.e., Talk to Frank or Drinkaware] website says that _____ [insert relevant information for the substance].
We could look together at information related to this the next time we meet; what do you think?
For more information, you can look on the _____ [insert name of the website—i.e., Talk to Frank or Drinkaware] website.

▶ Worksheet 1: What Do I Enjoy About Using or What Keeps Me Using?

What I enjoy about using _____ [insert name of the substance], or what keeps me using _____ [insert name of the substance]:

1. _____

2. _____

3. _____

4. _____

5. _____

When I look over my list, I feel _____

Looking at it, does it make me think differently?

_____

The most important benefit or biggest plus of using _____ [insert name of the substance] has been _____.

Taking another look?

When I took another look at the good things I tend to think about _____ [insert name of the substance], I noticed that using sometimes has different effects than I expect, such as _____

Looking at it now, does it make me think differently?

_____

Difficulties my use may be causing?

1. _____

2. _____

3. _____

4. _____

5. _____

When I look over my list I feel _____

Looking at it, does it make me think differently?
_____

So, when I sum up the *main concerns*, it is that my use
may_____

To *reduce the level of concern*, I would need to_____
_____

▶ Worksheet 2: What I Enjoy About Using or What Keeps Me Using (Table)

_____

[insert name of substance]

What I enjoy about using, or what keeps me using?	Difficulties my substance use may be causing?

When I look over my list, I feel _____

Looking at it, does my list make me think differently?

_____

The most important benefit or biggest plus of using _____ [insert name of the substance] has been _____

When I took another look at the good things I tend to think about _____ [insert name of the substance]. I noticed that using sometimes has different effects than I expect, such as _____

So, when I sum up the *main concerns*, it is that my use may

_____

To *reduce the level of concern*, I would need to

_____

▶ Worksheet 3: How Does My Use Sometimes Affect Me?

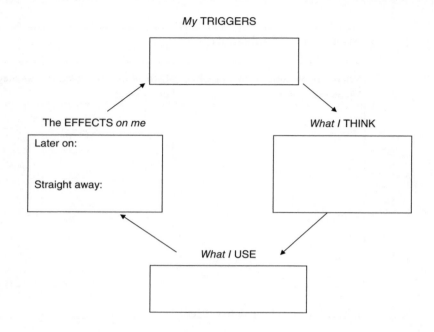

My TRIGGERS

The EFFECTS on me

Later on:

Straight away:

What I THINK

What I USE

▶ Worksheet 4: Taking Steps Toward My Goal

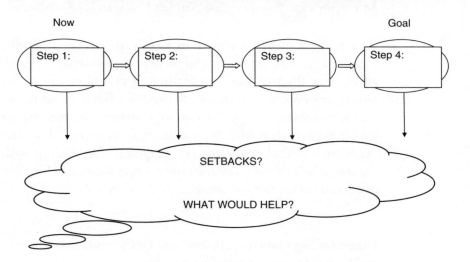

Now

Step 1:

Step 2:

Step 3:

Step 4:

Goal

SETBACKS?

WHAT WOULD HELP?

▶ Handout 1: Helpful Information for Family Members or Supportive Social Network Members

This section provides strategies that will encourage family members or supportive social network members to think about how the situation is affecting them and others in the family or network in terms of the stresses faced. In addition, family members or supportive social network members will be encouraged to consider the range of feelings that they are experiencing, and strategies are suggested for dealing with these in a helpful way. The following information can be given as a handout for family members or close friends.

Understanding Cannabis, Alcohol, and Other Substance Use, and How It Impacts on Family and Others

This information section is aimed at helping you understand and respond to the challenging experience of having someone close to you who experiences substance misuse and mental health problems, and to think about ways in which you can look after yourself as well as offer support to the person you are concerned about. If you are reading this, it is more than likely that a friend or loved one has developed a problem with substance use in addition to mental health problems. On the other hand, you may be unsure about whether there is a problem, whether the problem is a serious one, and yet you are worried. Finding out that your relative has got a substance problem is unlikely to happen as a single event. You may have been wondering for a while if he or she has been using drugs. Perhaps his or her behavior has at times been unpredictable or changeable in ways that are difficult to explain or fully understand. We also know that, when substance use problems also happen alongside mental health problems, this combination can be complex and challenging.

Let us focus on your experience to start with. We know from research and from what family members or supportive social network members have told us that their experiences can include, for example, being concerned about the person's health and safety, the financial implications of drug use, finding the person difficult to live with, incidents and crises at home, and a lot of worry about the impact on family or friendships. All of these are common experiences that families describe at some length when asked about living with a close relative with a substance use problem or a substance use and mental health problem combined.

One of the most important things to keep in mind as a family member or a supportive social network member in these situations is to not panic. It is likely that, in time, you can find a way of understanding what is happening that will be helpful. A good starting point is to understand your own experience, as this is mostly within your control (although at times it may not feel like this!).

Do Others Experience Similar Problems?

Before thinking and looking more closely at your own experience, it is worth considering how common these problems are. Living with someone with a drug or alcohol problem is a very common experience. It happens to a lot of people, although it is mostly hidden because people do not like to talk about this to others. A common feeling reported by family members or supportive friends is shame and worry about what other people may think of the person who is using the drugs, of you, or of the family as a whole. If you feel like this, it is problematic, because it will make you hide the experience and increase your isolation. In addition, we know that disagreements can take place between different family members or friends when these problems are discussed. This again can increase your sense of hopelessness and isolation and the feeling that you are dealing with this problem on your own, which in turn can be a really challenging experience. In fact, living with someone with a substance misuse problem and being affected by this experience is so common that it ranks among the most commonly reported forms of severe and chronic stress within the Western world. Here, we are talking about millions of people rather than thousands. In fact, in a recent study we conducted, we estimated that there are over 1 million adult family members significantly affected by the serious drug problem, including cannabis, of someone in the family in the United Kingdom.

The number increases exponentially if we consider alcohol problems as well. Hence, one of the most important things to remind yourself, if you are feeling like this, is that *YOU ARE NOT ALONE.*

How Do I Make Sense of This?

Having established that this is a common experience, as we were saying earlier, it is important to think about the aspects of the experience that can be under your control even though they may not feel controllable at present. Gaining some sense of control and understanding of your experience will help you feel less confused, and will allow you to identify and name some of the roller coaster of emotions that you may be feeling at present (e.g., anger, despair, and fear). Being able to name those emotions and identify why they are happening and where they come from can make you feel better even when the drug problem of your relative has not changed much or at all. First, you can try and identify a situation or behavior related to your experience, for example, your son coming back home late at night and appearing quite confused and "stoned." Describe the event as clearly and specifically as you can (e.g., Martin comes home very late and appears to be "stoned"). You may even go onto describe some of the signs that make you think this (e.g., he is giddy, does not make sense, and his eyes look very puffy). Next, try to identify what you felt when this happened. Again, try and be very specific (e.g., "I feel really *annoyed* when this happens but also *frightened* and *upset*," as opposed to "I feel like my world is collapsing," which is a rather broad and abstract description). In the first example, you are naming the feelings and making them clear, the first step toward dealing with them. You can also explore some of those feelings in more depth. You can try and think about what you are frightened of, or about what is making you feel upset. For example, we know that a lot of family members or supportive social network members fear for the health and safety of their loved one and feel upset because they feel let down and feel that they cannot trust the person.

At times, you may start wondering whether the only positive thing that can happen is that your loved one seeks help for his or her alcohol or drug use. While this would clearly be a very positive step, it may not happen for a while. However, we know that family members or supportive friends can improve their experience and come to terms with some of the feelings of despair by working on their own understanding of the situation, even in those cases where the person does not access help straightaway or change in the short term. It may also be important at this stage for you to consider what the impact is on other members of the family or network of friends of the person using alcohol or drugs.

Why Do I Feel So Stressed?

The next area that is important to consider at this early stage is the *strains* that you, as a family member or a friend, may be experiencing. We know that family members of people with addiction problems have high symptoms of physical and psychological stress. Physical symptoms include experiences such as loss of appetite, difficulty sleeping, and high blood pressure. Psychological symptoms include feeling anxious or depressed, increasing your own intake of substances by drinking or smoking more, and a general sense of worry that is with you most of the time. However, starting to talk to people who are in a position to help may be a very important first step for you to take. Being able to make sense of your experience may allow you to help and support your loved one from a calmer and positive stance.

To Sum It Up

If you have read up to this point, we hope that this would have helped you to think more about your situation and the problems that you are facing. We hope also that you have been able to identify more specifically and clearly the aspects of the situation that are contributing to your experience of stress and worry, and also considered some of the possible symptoms of stress that you are experiencing as an affected family member or close friend. This is a very important step in order to begin to take control of your situation and your experience, and to plan ways of responding to both your needs and those of your loved one in a helpful way.

The most important thing to remind yourself is that *YOU ARE NOT ALONE*, that there are millions of other people experiencing similar situations, and that some of the most frightening thoughts and feelings you have had are the result of the stress that is arising from your understandable concern and worry about your loved one. Beginning to come to grips with what is going on for yourself and for your relative or friend is the first step in planning what to do in response.

Depending on where you live, there will be organizations that offer support and, in some parts of the world, self-help groups for family members affected by the drug and mental health problems of a relative. In the United Kingdom and other countries, for example, there will be Al-Anon groups supporting families dealing with alcohol misuse and Families Anonymous groups supporting families dealing with drug misuse. Adfam, again in the United Kingdom, is a national organization working in a range of ways to support families affected by drug use and can offer advice about local services.

Some books that you may be interested in reading
Mueser, K. T. & Gingerich, S. (2006). *The Complete Family Guide to Schizophrenia: Helping Your Loved One Get the Most Out of Life.* New York: Guilford Press. This book is focused on schizophrenia and has an excellent section devoted to the use of alcohol and drugs in those with severe mental health problems.

Books that cover the impact of drug and alcohol use on families and different family members
Barnard, M. (2007). *Drug Addiction and Families.* London: Jessica Kingsley.
Orford, J. (2012). *Addiction Dilemmas. Family Experiences in Literature and Research and Their Lessons for Practice.* Chichester: Wiley-Blackwell.
Trimingham, T. (2009). *Not My Family, Never My Child: What Do To If Someone You Love Is a Drug User.* Australia: Allen & Unwin.

You will be able to find additional resources quoted in these books or related websites.

▶ Handout 2: How Can I Best Support My Family Member or Friend?

Keeping Communication Open

Your family member, loved one, or friend may have approached you as someone who he or she thinks can offer support to make a change or achieve an identified important goal. This can be helpful for both yourself and the person with the substance misuse and mental health problem, as it means that you will be able to communicate more openly with each other, and you may be able to offer your support and encouragement, which we know is important in helping people change substance use habits and achieve their goals. Keeping communication open is an important aim.

Supporting His or Her Goals

Listen to what your loved one may tell you about his or her goals, and talk together if necessary with help from your loved one's Clinician about the possible ways in which you may support his or her goal. Your loved one's goals may involve, for example, trying to "avoid admission to a mental health unit in the future," and part of this may involve trying to not use substances. Other goals may involve personal aims—for example, getting a job, learning to drive, or getting fitter. Your loved one will be encouraged to identify a small, realistic, substance-related or personal goal, and to think about people who are important and can offer support in achieving this goal. You can support this goal at the simplest level by being genuinely encouraging or, at a more practical level, by helping him or her identify and pursue ways of achieving the goal—for example, visiting the job center together or exploring together ways of increasing physical exercise and getting fitter.

References

Arseneault, L., Cannon, M., Poulton, R., Murray, R., Caspi, A. & Moffitt, T. E. (2002). Cannabis use in adolescence and risk for adult psychosis: longitudinal prospective study. *BMJ*, **325**, 1212–1213. doi: 10.1136/bmj.325.7374.1212.

Baker, A. L., Kavanagh, D. J., Kay-Lambkin, F. J., Hunt, S. A., Lewin, T. J., Carr, V. J. & Connolly, J. (2009). Randomized controlled trial of cognitive-behavioural therapy for coexisting depression and alcohol problems: short-term outcome. *Addiction*, **105**, 87–99. doi:10.1111/j.1360-0443.2009.02757.x.

Barnard, M. (2007). *Drug Addiction and Families*. London: Jessica Kingsley.

Beck, A. T., Wright, F., Newman, C. & Liese, B. (1993). *Cognitive Therapy of Substance Abuse*. New York: Guilford Press.

Brabban, A. & Turkington, D. (2002). The search for meaning: detecting congruence between life events, underlying schema and psychotic symptoms. In A. P. Morrison (ed.), *A Casebook of Cognitive Therapy for Psychosis* (Chapter 5, pp. 59–75). New York: Brunner-Routledge.

Buchbinder, M., Wilbur, R., Zuskov, D., Mclean, S. & Sleath, B. (2014). Teachable moments and missed opportunities for smoking cessation counselling in a hospital emergency department: a mixed-methods study of patient-provider communication. *BMC Health Services Research*, **14**, 651.

Carey, K. B. (1996). Substance use reduction in the context of outpatient psychiatric treatment: A collaborative, motivational, harm reduction approach. *Community Mental Health Journal*, **32**(3), 291–306. doi: 10.1007/BF02249430.

Carey, K. B., Carey, M. P., Maisto, S. A. & Purnine, D. M. (2002). The feasibility of enhancing psychiatric outpatients' readiness to

Brief Integrated Motivational Intervention: A Treatment Manual for Co-occurring Mental Health and Substance Use Problems, First Edition. Hermine L. Graham, Alex Copello, Max Birchwood, and Emma Griffith.
© 2016 John Wiley & Sons, Ltd. Published 2016 by John Wiley & Sons, Ltd.
Companion Website: www.wiley.com/go/graham/bimi

change their substance use. *Psychiatric Services*, **53**, 602–608. doi: 10.1176/appi.ps.53.5.602.

Copello, A., Orford, J., Hodgson, R. & Tober, G. (2009). *Social Behaviour and Network Therapy for Alcohol Problems*. London: Routledge.

Crown Copyright (2009a). Cannabis: Too much too often. Retrieved from: www.talktofrank.com/sites/default/files/cannabistmto.pdf

Crown Copyright (2009b). Cannabis: Cannabis find out the facts. Retrieved from: www.talktofrank.com/sites/default/files/Cannabis%20Find%20Out%20The%20Facts.pdf

Department of Health (DOH) (2002). *Mental Health Policy Implementation Guide: Dual Diagnosis Good Practice Guide*. London: DOH.

Department of Health (DOH) (2006). Dual diagnosis in mental health inpatient and day hospital settings. Retrieved from: www.dh.gov.uk/en/Publicationsandstatistics/Publications/PublicationsPolicyAndGuidance/DH_062649.

Di Forti, M., Sallis, H., Allegri, F., Trotta, A., Ferraro, L., Stilo, S. A., Marconi, A., La Cascia, C., Reis Marques, T., Pariante, C., Dazzan, P., Mondelli, V., Paparelli, A., Kolliakou, A., Prata, D., Gaughran, F., David, A. S., Morgan, C., Stahl, D., Khondoker, M., MacCabe, J. H. & Murray, R. M. (2014). Daily use, especially of high-potency cannabis, drives the earlier onset of psychosis in cannabis users. *Schizophrenia Bulletin*, **40**(6), 1509–1517.

Dragt, S., Nieman, D. H., Schultze-Lutter, F., van der Meer, F., Becker, H., de Haan, L., Dingemans, P. M., Birchwood, M., Patterson, P., Salokangas, R. K., Heinimaa, M., Heinz, A., Juckel, G., Graf von Reventlow, H., French, P., Stevens, H., Ruhrmann, S., Klosterkötter, J. & Linszen, D. H. (2012). Cannabis use and age at onset of symptoms in subjects at clinical high risk for psychosis. *Acta Psychiatrica Scandinavica*, **125**, 45–53. doi: 10.1111/j.1600-0447.2011.01763.x.

Drake, R. E., Essock, S. M., Shaner, A., Carey, K. B., Minkoff, K., Kola, L., Lynde, D., Osher, F. C., Clark, R. E. & Rickards, L. (2001). Implementing dual diagnosis services for clients with severe mental illness. *Psychiatric Services*, **52**, 469–476. doi: 10.1176/appi.ps.52.4.469.

Drinkaware (2013). Why use MyDrinkaware. Retrieved from: www.drinkaware.co.uk/unitcalculator

Drinkaware (2015a). Alcohol and mental health. Retrieved from: www.drinkaware.co.uk/check-the-facts/health-effects-of-alcohol/mental-health/alcohol-and-mental-health

Drinkaware (2015b). Alcohol unit guidelines. Retrieved from: www.drinkaware.co.uk/check-the-facts/what-is-alcohol/daily-guidelines

Drinkaware (2015c). Binge drinking. Retrieved from: www.drinkaware. co.uk/understand-your-drinking/is-your-drinking-a-problem/ binge-drinking

Drinkaware (2015d). Calories in alcohol. Retrieved from: www. drinkaware.co.uk/check-the-facts/health-effects-of-alcohol/ appearance/calories-in-alcohol

Drinkaware (2015e). Health effects of alcohol. Retrieved from: www. drinkaware.co.uk/check-the-facts/health-effects-of-alcohol

Edwards, J., Elkins, K., Hinton, M., Harrigan, S. M., Donovan, K., Athanasopoulos, O. & McGorry, P. D. (2006). Randomized controlled trial of a cannabis-focused intervention for young people with first-episode psychosis. *Acta Psychiatr Scand*, **114**(2), 109–117.

EMCDDA (2014). *European Drug Report: Trends and Developments*. Lisbon: EMCDDA.

Follette, V. M. & Pistorello, J. (2007). *Finding Life beyond Trauma: Using Acceptance and Commitment Therapy to Heal from Post-Traumatic Stress and Trauma-Related Problem*. Oakland, CA: New Harbinger Publications, Inc.

Genetic Risk and Outcome In Psychosis (GROUP) Investigators (2011). Evidence that familial liability for psychosis is expressed as differential sensitivity to cannabis. An analysis of patient-sibling and sibling-control pairs. *Archives of General Psychiatry*, **68**(2), 138–147.

Gossop, M., Darke, S., Griffiths, P., Hando, J., Powis, B., Hall, W. & Strang, J. (1995). The Severity of Dependence Scale (SDS): psychometric properties of the SDS in English and Australian samples of heroin, cocaine and amphetamine users. *Addiction*, **90**(5), 607–614.

Graham, H. L., Maslin, J., Copello, A., Birchwood, M., Mueser, K., McGovern, D. & Georgiou, G. (2001). Drug and alcohol problems amongst individuals with severe mental health problems in an inner city area of the United Kingdom. *Social Psychiatry and Psychiatric Epidemiology*, **36**, 448–455.

Graham, H. L., Copello, A., Birchwood, M. J., Mueser, K. T., Orford, J., McGovern, D., Atkinson, E., Maslin, J., Preece, M., Tobin, D. & Georgiou, G. (2004). *Cognitive-Behavioural Integrated Treatment (C-BIT): A Treatment Manual for Substance Misuse in People with Severe Mental Health Problems*. Chichester: Wiley & Sons.

Graham, H. L., Copello, A., Birchwood, M., Griffith, E., Freemantle, N., McCrone, P., Clarke, L., Walsh, K., Stefanidou, C. A., Rana, A. (2016). Pilot randomised trial of a brief intervention for co-morbid substance misuse in psychiatric inpatient settings. *Acta Psychiatrica Scandinavica*, **133**(4), 298–309.

Greenberger, D. & Padesky, C. (1995). *Mind Over Mood*. Basingstoke: Guilford Press.

Hayes, S. C. (2005). *Get Out of Your Mind and Into Your Life: The New Acceptance and Commitment Therapy*. Oakland, CA: New Harbinger Publications, Inc.

Healthcare Commission (2008). The pathway to recovery: a review of NHS acute inpatient mental health services. *Commission for Healthcare Audit and Inspection*, 1–92.

Hettema, J., Steele, J. & Miller, W. R. (2005). Motivational interviewing. *Annual Review of Clinical Psychology*, **1**, 91–111. doi: 10.1146/annurev.clinpsy.1.102803.143833.

Home Office (2013). *Drug Misuse: Findings from the 2012 to 2013 Crime Survey for England and Wales*. London, United Kingdom: The Home Office. Available at: www.gov.uk/government/publications/drug-misuse-findings-from-the-2012-to-2013-csew/drug-misuse-findings-from-the-2012-to-2013-crime-survey-for-england-and-wales

Hunt, G. E., Siegfried, N., Morley, K., Sitharthan, T. & Cleary, M. (2013). Psychosocial interventions for people with both severe mental illness and substance misuse. *Cochrane Database of Systematic Reviews*, (10). Art. No.: CD001088. DOI: 10.1002/14651858.CD001088.pub3.

Kavanagh, D. J., Young, R., White, A., Saunders, J. B., Wallis, J., Shockley, N., Jenner, L. & Clair, A. (2004). A brief integrated motivational intervention for substance misuse in recent-onset psychosis. *Drug and Alcohol Review*, **23**, 151–155. doi: 10.1080/09595230410001704127.

Kay-Lambkin, F. J., Baker, A. L., Kelly, B. J., Lewin, T. J. & Carr, V. J. (2008). Randomized controlled trial of computerized cognitive behaviour therapy for depression and substance use comorbidity. *Australian and New Zealand Journal of Psychiatry, Newcastle, NSW*.

Konings, M., Henquet, C., Maharajh, H., Hutchinson, G. & Van Os, J. (2008). Early exposure to cannabis and risk of psychosis in young adolescents in Trinidad. *Acta Psychiatrica Scandanavia*, **118**, 209–213.

Kroenke, K., Spitzer, R. L. & Williams, J. B. W. (2001). The PHQ-9: validity of a brief depression severity measure. *Journal of General Internal Medicine*, **16**, 606–613.

Lai, H. M. & Sitharthan, T. (2012). Comparison of inpatients with comorbid mental health disorders and alcohol-and other-substance-use disorders within general hospitals and psychiatric hospitals in NSW, Australia. *Journal of Substance Use*, **17**(3), 301–309.

Large, M., Sharma, S., Compton, M. T., Slade, T. & Nielssen, O. (2011). Cannabis use and earlier onset of psychosis: a systematic meta-analysis. *Archives of General Psychiatry*, **68**(6), 555.

Lau, K., Freyer-Adam, J., Gaertner B., Rumpf, H. J., John, U. & Hapke, U. (2010). Motivation to change risky drinking and motivation to seek help for alcohol risk drinking among general hospital inpatients with problem drinking and alcohol-related diseases. *General Hospital Psychiatry*, **32**(1), 86–93.

Macneil, C. A., Hasty, M. K., Conus, P., Berk, M. & Scott, J. (2009). Bipolar Disorder in young people: a psychological intervention manual. Cambridge: Cambridge University Press.

Marsden, J., Gossop, M., Stewart, D., Best, D., Farrell, M. & Strang, J. (1998). The Maudsley addiction profile: a brief instrument for treatment outcome research. National Addiction Centre/Institute of Psychiatry, United Kingdom.

McGrath, J., Welham, J., Scott, J., Varghese, D., Degenhardt, L., Hayatbakhsh, M., Alati, R., Williams, G. M., Bor, W. & Najman, J. (2010). Sibling-pair analysis confirms an association between cannabis use and psychosis-related outcomes in a cohort of young adults. *Archives of General Psychiatry*, **67**(5), 440–447. doi: 10.1093/schbul/sbq173.

McHugo, G. J., Drake, R. E., Burton, H. L. & Ackerson, T. H. (1995). A scale for assessing the stage of substance abuse treatment in persons with severe mental illness. *The Journal of Nervous and Mental Disease*, **183**, 762–767.

Mueser, K. T. (2003). Integrated service delivery models. In H. L. Graham, A. Copello, K. T. Birchwood, M. J. Mueser (ed.), *Substance Misuse in Psychosis: Approaches to Treatment and Service Delivery* (pp. 93–105). Chichester: Wiley & Sons.

Mueser, K. T. & Gingerich, S. (2006). *The Complete Family Guide to Schizophrenia: Helping Your Loved One Get the Most Out of Life*. New York: Guilford Press.

Mueser, K. T., Bellack, A. S. & Blanchard, J. J. (1992). Co-morbidity of schizophrenia and substance abuse: implications for treatment. *Journal of Consulting and Clinical Psychology*, **60**, 845–856.

Mueser, K. T., Yarnold, P. R., Rosenberg, S. D., Swett, C., Miles, K. M. & Hill, D. (2000). Substance use disorder in hospitalized severely mentally ill psychiatric patients: prevalence, correlates, and subgroups. *Schizophrenia Bulletin*, **26**, 179–192.

National Institute for Health and Clinical Excellence (2011). *Psychosis with Coexisting Substance Misuse: Assessment and Management in Adults and Young People*. London: The British Psychological Society and The Royal College of Psychiatrists.

NHS Choices (2014a). Binge drinking. Retrieved from:www.nhs.uk/Livewell/alcohol/Pages/Bingedrinking.aspx

NHS Choices (2014b). Calories in alcohol. Retrieved from:www.nhs.uk/Livewell/alcohol/Pages/calories-in-alcohol.aspx

NHS Choices (2015). Alcohol units. Retrieved from: www.nhs.uk/Livewell/alcohol/Pages/alcohol-units.aspx#table

NHS Statistics on Alcohol England (2011). *Statistics on Alcohol: England, 2011*. Leeds, United Kingdom: The Health and Social Care Information Centre, Lifestyles Statistics. Available at: https://catalogue.ic.nhs.uk/publications/public-health/alcohol/alco-eng-2011/alco-eng-2011-rep.pdf

NHS Statistics on Drug Misuse England (2012). *Statistics on Drug Misuse: England, 2012*. Leeds, United Kingdom: The Health and Social Care Information Centre, Lifestyles Statistics. Available at: https://catalogue.ic.nhs.uk/publications/public-health/drug-misuse/drug-misu-eng-2012/drug-misu-eng-2012-rep.pdf

Orford, J. (2012). *Addiction Dilemmas. Family Experiences in Literature and Research and Their Lessons for Practice*. Chichester: Wiley-Blackwell.

Regier, D. A., Farmer, M. E., Rae, D. S., Locke, B. Z., Keith, S. J., Judd, L. L. & Goodwin, F. K. (1990). Comorbidity of mental disorders with alcohol and other drug abuse: results from the Epidemiologic Catchment Area (ECA) Study. *Journal of American Medical Association*, **264**, 2511–2518. doi: 10.1001/jama.1990.03450190043026.

Rollnick, S., Butler, C. C. & Stott, N. (1997). Helping smokers make decisions: the enhancement of brief intervention for general medical practice. *Patient Education and Counseling*, **31**, 191–203.

Saunders, J. B., Aasland, O. G., Babor, T. F., Fuente, J. R. & Grant, M. (1993). Development of the Alcohol Use Disorders Screening Test (AUDIT): WHO collaborative project on early detection of persons with harmful alcohol consumption: II. *Addiction*, **88**, 791–804.

Spitzer, R. L., Kroenke, K., Williams, J. B. W. & Löwe, B. (2006). A brief measure for assessing generalized anxiety disorder: the GAD-7. Archives of Internal Medicine, **166**, 1092–1097.

Spitzer, R. L., Williams, J. B. W., Kroenke, K., Linzer, M., deGruy, F. V., Hahn, S. R., Brody, D. & Johnson, J. G. (1994). Utility of a new procedure for diagnosing mental disorders in primary care: The PRIME-MD 1000 study. *Journal of the American Medical Association*, **272**, 1749–1756.

Swanson, A. J., Pantalon, M. V. & Cohen, K. R. (1999). Motivational interviewing and treatment adherence among psychiatric and dually diagnosed clients. *Journal of Nervous and Mental Disorders*, **187**, 630–635. doi: 10.1097/00005053-199910000-00007.

Swartz, M. S., Wagner, H. R., Swanson, J. W., Stroup, T. S., McEvoy, J. P., Canive, J. M., Miller, D. D., Reimherr, F., McGee, M., Khan, A., Van Dorn, R., Rosenheck, R. A. & Lieberman, J. A. (2006). Substance use in persons with schizophrenia: baseline prevalence and correlates from the NIMH CATIE study. *The Journal of Nervous and Mental Disease*, **194**, 164–172.

Tait, L., Birchwood, M. & Trower, P. (2003). Predicting engagement with services for psychosis: insight, symptoms and recovery style. *British Journal of Psychiatry*, **182**, 123–128. doi: 10.1192/bjp.02.252

Talk to Frank (2011). Cannabis. Retrieved from: www.talktofrank.com/drug/cannabis

Talk to Frank (2013a). Alcohol: The drug, the effects, the risks. Retrieved from: www.talktofrank.com/drug/alcohol

Talk to Frank (2013b). Cocaine: The drug, the effects, the risks. Retrieved from: www.talktofrank.com/drug/cocaine#aka=Crack

Trimingham, T. (2009). *Not My Family, Never My Child: What To Do If Someone You Love Is a Drug User*. Australia: Allen & Unwin.

Van Os, J., Kenis, G. & Rutten, B. P. F. (2010). The environment and schizophrenia. *Nature*, **468**, 203–212.

Zubin, J. & Spring, B. (1977). Vulnerability: a new view of schizophrenia. *Journal of Abnormal Psychology*, **86**, 103–126.

Index

Page numbers in *italics* refer to figures, blank worksheets and sample questionnaires. Page numbers in **bold** refer to tables and blank questionnaires.

aims of BIMI
   Booster Session 85–86
   FAQs 42
   overall aims 3, 4–5, 9
   session goals **6, 7**
   STEP 1 9, 10
   STEP 2 56
   STEP 3 69–70
Alcohol Use Disorders
     Identification Test
     (AUDIT)
   case examples 24–25, **27**,
     39, 41
   how to use it 12–13
   score sheet **16, 92**
   when to use it 22
   in Your Results sheet 32, 33,
     35, 96
anxiety assessment (GAD-7)
     13–14, 19, **19**, 23–24, **30**,
     95, **95**
approach, BIMI 4

assessment session *see* STEP 1
     (Engagement and Brief
     Assessment)
assessment sheets, blank
   AUDIT **16, 92**
   BIMI Brief Assessment **15,
     90–91**
   GAD-7 **19, 95**
   Importance–Confidence
     Ruler **17, 93**
   PHQ-9 **18, 94**
   SDS **17, 93**
   Your Results **35, 96**

"benefits" of using 57–61
between sessions 7
BIMI Brief Assessment sheet **15,
   90–91**
Booster Session
   community-based services 89
   revisiting earlier sessions 86
   maintenance cycle 87–88

Brief Integrated Motivational Intervention: A Treatment Manual for Co-occurring Mental Health and Substance Use Problems, First Edition. Hermine L. Graham, Alex Copello, Max Birchwood, and Emma Griffith.
© 2016 John Wiley & Sons, Ltd. Published 2016 by John Wiley & Sons, Ltd.
Companion Website: www.wiley.com/go/graham/bimi

Booster Session (*cont'd*)
    self-motivational statements
      of concern and intention
      to change 86–87
    skills to tackle setbacks 88
    social support for
      change 88–89
    substance-related goals 88
    session content/goals overview
      7, **85**, 85–86
    timing 85
brief Integrated Motivational
    Intervention (BIMI)
    assessment *see* STEP 1
    (Engagement and Brief
    Assessment)
BIMI Brief Assessment
    12–14, 19
BIMI Brief Assessment sheet
    15–19

case examples
    Crystal (paranoid psychosis/
      cocaine) 25–26, **26–30**, *41*
    Sam (schizophrenia/
      cannabis) 19–24, *38*
    Sebastian (bipolar affective
      disorder/alcohol)
      24–25, *39–40*
C-BIT (Cognitive-Behavioural
    Integrated Treatment) 3
cognitive behavioural therapy
    (CBT) 3, 59
cognitive distortions 59
community-based services 7,
    76, 85–86, 89
content, session **6**, **7**
coping strategies 72–75
"costs" of using 62–68; *see also*
    substance use/misuse,
    impact on mental health
cravings/urges, coping
    with 72–75

depression assessment
    GAD-7 13–14, 19, **19**, 23–24,
      30, 95, **95**
    PHQ-9 13–14, **18**, 19, 22–23,
      29, 31, **94**, 95
distraction coping strategy 73
*Do Others Experience Similar
    Problems?* handout 80,
    102–103
Drinkaware website
    binge drinking 43, 44
    daily guidelines 43
    drink diary 43
    health effects 46
    units and calories calculator
      32, 45
    using information in case
      examples 34, **35**, *39*, *40*
    using information to answer
      FAQs 43, 44
duration of sessions 4

engagement
    building *see* STEP 1
      (Engagement and Brief
      Assessment)
    for change *see* STEP 2
      (Decisions about
      Change)
    conversational style 11
    factors affecting 2, 3
    importance for success 3
    timing 4–5;
    see also relationship with
      client, collaborative

family members *see* social
    networks, supportive
feedback to clients 5, 10; *see also*
    Your Results sheets
Frequently Asked Questions
    (FAQs) 36
    aims and overview 42–43

example questions
    alcohol 43–46
    drugs and mental health
        46–51
    getting better 51–52
friends *see* social networks,
        supportive

Generalized Anxiety Disorder
        (GAD-7) questionnaire
        13–14, **19**, 19, 23–24, **30**,
        95, **95**
goals, client's self-identified 4
goals, session **6**, **7**

handouts for family/friends
    *Do Others Experience
        Similar Problems?* 80,
        102–103
    *How Can I Best Support My
        Family Member or
        Friend?* 83–84, 106
    How Do I Make Sense of This?
        80–81, 103–104
    To Sum It Up 82–83,
        104–105
    *Understanding Cannabis,
        Alcohol, and Other
        Substance Use, and How It
        Impacts on Family and
        Others* 79, 101–102
    Why Do I Feel So Stressed?
        81–82, 104
    *How Can I Best Support My Family
        Member or Friend?*
        handout 83–84, 106
    "How Does My Use
        Sometimes Affect Me?"
        worksheet 60–68, 72,
        86, *100*
    How Do I Make Sense of This?
        handout 80–81,
        103–104

imagery coping strategy 73, 75
Importance–Confidence Ruler
        13, **17**, 22, **28**, 53, **93**
intention to change 86, 87

maintenance cycle 64, 87–88
Maudsley Addiction Profile
        (MAP) 12, **15**, 20–21, **26**,
        90–91
mental health
    assessing
        GAD-7 13–14, **19**, 19,
            23–24, **30**, **95**, 95
        PHQ-9 13–14, **18**,
            19, 22–23, **29**, 31,
            94, 95
    FAQs 46–51
    hope to get better 51–52
    impact of substance use/
        misuse 2, 34, 46–51,
        62–68, 87–88
    stress-vulnerability model *47*,
        47–48
motivational interviewing 3
motivation to change
    assessing 13, **17**, 53, **93**
    case examples *38, 39, 41*
    in Your Results sheet 33,
        35, **96**

number of BIMI sessions 4

overview of BIMI 3–5, **6**, **7**, 7

Patient Health Questionnaire
        (PHQ-9) 13–14, **18**, 19,
        22–23, **29**, 31, **94**, 95
Personalized Assessment
        Feedback sheets *see* Your
        Results sheets
precontemplators 1
psychoeducational materials/
        leaflets 5, 7, 34, 36, 62

questionnaires
  AUDIT
    case examples 24–25, **27**, *39, 41*
    how to use it 12–13
    score sheet **16**, **92**
    when to use it 22
    in Your Results sheet 32, 33, **35**, **96**
  GAD-7 13–14, **19**, 19, 23–24, **30**, **95**, 95
  Importance–Confidence Ruler 13, **17**, 22, **28**, 53, **93**
  MAP 12, **15**, 20–21, **26**, **90–91**
  PHQ-9 13–14, **18**, 19, 22–23, **29**, 31, **94**, 95
  SDS
    blank form **17**, **93**
    case examples 26, **28**
    how to use it 13
    when to use it 22
    in Your Results sheet 32, 33, **35**, **96**
  using
    case example: Crystal 25–26, **26–30**, *41*
    case example: Sam 19–24, *38*
    case example: Sebastian 24–25, *39–40*

relationship with client
  collaborative 4, 10, 11, 30–31, 76, 78
  conversational style 4, 11
  mindset of health worker 8
  non-judgmental 10, 11, 24–25, 36
relaxation coping strategy 73

sealing over experiences 3
sessions, BIMI
  duration 4
  number 4

structure 5, 7; *see also specific STEP*
timing 4–5
setbacks, coping with 72–73, 74–75, 88, *100*
Severity of Dependence Scale (SDS) questionnaire
  blank form **17**, **93**
  case examples 26, **28**
  how to use it 13
  when to use it 22
  in Your Results sheet 32, 33, **35**, **96**
social networks, supportive
  diagram 76–78, *77*
  handouts for family/friends *see* handouts for family/friends
  importance for success 75–76
  reviewing 88–89
Spring, B. 47
statements of concern, self-motivational 86, 87
STEP 1 (Engagement and Brief Assessment)
  session content/goals overview **6**, **9**
  session one
    aims 10
    AUDIT 12–13, **16**, 24–25, **27**
    BIMI Brief Assessment 12–14, 19
    BIMI Brief Assessment sheet **15–19**
    case example: Crystal 25–26, **26–30**
    case example: Sam 19–24
    case example: Sebastian 24–25
    client's participation/involvement 30–31
    GAD-7 13–14, 14–15, **19**, 23–24, **30**

Importance–Confidence
	Ruler 13, **17**, 22, **28**
MAP 12, 20–21, **26**
outline 10–11
overview 10
PHQ-9 13–14, **18**, 22–23,
	29, 31
SDS 13, **17**, 22, 26, **28**
setting up session two 31
session two
	client's participation/
		involvement 37
	FAQs *see* Frequently Asked
		Questions (FAQs)
	outline 36–37
	overview 36
	Your Results sheet **35**
	Your Results sheet,
		Crystal's *41*
	Your Results sheet,
		generating 31–34
	Your Results sheet,
		Sam's *38*
	Your Results sheet,
		Sebastian's *39–40*
	therapist's state of mind 8
STEP 2 (Decisions about
	Change)
	"benefits" of using 57–58,
		59–60
	"costs" of using 65–68
	mental health-substance use
		relationship 62–65
	positive thoughts and
		mis-held beliefs 58–59
	re-evaluating thoughts/
		beliefs 60–61
	session content/goals
		overview **6**, 56, **56**
	worksheets 1 and 2 57–60,
		61, 66, 67, 68, 86,
		97–98, *99*
	worksheet 3 60–68, 72,
		86, *100*

STEP 3 (Change Plans and
	Social Support)
	coping strategies 72–75
	information for family/
		friends 78–84
	session content/goals
		overview **6**, *69*,
		69–70
	social networks 75–78, *77*
	"Taking Steps Toward My
		Goal" worksheet
		71–72, *100*
STEPS, deciding on 53,
	54, 55
stressors *47*, 47–48
stress-vulnerability model *47*,
	47–48
structure of BIMI 5, **6**, **7**, *7*;
		see also specific STEP
substance-related goals 88
substance use/misuse
	assessing *see* STEP 1
		(Engagement and Brief
		Assessment)
	"benefits" 57–61
	changing *see* STEP 2
		(Decisions about
		Change); STEP 3 (Change
		Plans and Social Support)
	"costs" 62–68
	FAQs *see* Frequently Asked
		Questions (FAQs)
	impact on mental health 2,
		34, 46–51, 62–68,
		87–88
	information for family/
		friends *see* handouts for
		family/friends
	motivation to change
		see motivation to
		change
	positive thoughts and
		mis-held beliefs 58–60
suicidal thoughts 23, 31

"Taking Steps Toward My Goal"
worksheet 63, 71–72, 86,
88, *100*
Talk to Frank website 7, 34, *38,*
40, 41, 49, 52
teachable moment 1, 5
therapist's state of mind 8
thinking errors 59
timing of BIMI 4–5
To Sum It Up handout 82–83,
104–105

Understanding Cannabis, Alcohol,
and Other Substance Use,
and How It Impacts on
Family and Others
handout 79, 101–102

vulnerabilities *47,* 47–48

websites
companion to book xi
Drinkaware *see* Drinkaware
website
encouraging clients to access
7, 36, 37, 52
mental health
questionnaires 14
PHQ Screeners 14
recognized/reliable 34
Talk to Frank 7, 34, *38, 40,*
41, 49, 52
Youth Space 52

"What Do I Enjoy About Using
or What Keeps Me
Using?" worksheets 1
and 2 57–60, 61, 66, 67,
68, 86, *97–98, 99*
Why Do I Feel So Stressed?
handout 81–82, 104
window of opportunity 1–3, 5
worksheets
"How Does My Use
Sometimes Affect
Me?" 60–68, 72,
86, *100*
"Taking Steps Toward My
Goal" 63, 71–72, 86,
88, *100*
"What Do I Enjoy About
Using or What Keeps
Me Using?" 57–60,
61, 66, 67, 68, 86,
97–98, 99

Your Results sheets
blank form **35**, **96**
case examples *38,*
39–40, 41
generating 31–34
reviewing with client *see* STEP
2 (Decisions about
Change)
Youth Space 52

Zubin, J. 47